the small heart of things

E S T. 75 1938
YEARS
THE UNIVERSITY OF GEORGIA PRESS 2013

the small heart of things

being at home in a beckoning world

JULIAN HOFFMAN

THE UNIVERSITY OF GEORGIA PRESS   *athens & london*

Paperback edition published in 2014 by
The University of Georgia Press
Athens, Georgia 30602
www.ugapress.org
© 2013 by Julian Hoffman
All rights reserved
Designed by Erin Kirk New
Set in Adobe Garamond Pro
Printed and bound by Sheridan Books
The paper in this book meets the guidelines for
permanence and durability of the Committee on
Production Guidelines for Book Longevity of the
Council on Library Resources.

Most University of Georgia Press titles are
available from popular e-book vendors.

Printed in the United States of America
18   17   16   15   14   P   5   4   3   2

The Library of Congress has cataloged the
hardcover edition of this book as follows:

Hoffman, Julian.
  The small heart of things : being at home in a beckoning
world / Julian Hoffman.
    xiii, 154 pages ; 23 cm. — (Association of Writers and Writing Programs
Award for Creative Nonfiction)
    ISBN-13: 978-0-8203-4556-7 (hardcover : alk. paper)
    ISBN-10: 0-8203-4556-3 (hardcover : alk. paper)
    PS3608.O47824S63 2013
    814'.6—dc23   2012048323

Paperback ISBN 978-0-8203-4757-8

British Library Cataloging-in-Publication Data available

FOR JULIA,

the heart of home

"You must come with no intentions of discovery.
You must overhear things, as though you'd come
into a small and desolate town and paused by
an open window."

BARRY LOPEZ, *Desert Notes*

"From the depths of mystery, and even from the
heights of splendor, we bounce back and hurry for
the latitudes of home."

ANNIE DILLARD, "Total Eclipse"

CONTENTS

PREFACE

PLACE HAS A PROFOUND bearing upon our lives, from the countries we are born into, or end up inhabiting, to the light, landscape, and weather peculiar to our home regions. Each has a say in shaping our cultures and souls. Greeks living in Athens and Thessaloníki, or any of the country's other large urban centers, usually have ties to somewhere else. If you were to ask them where they were from, rarely would they reply with the name of the city, even if it was the place where they were born and raised. Instead they would name a village, one among thousands scattered across the countryside and islands, the place of their forefathers and origins, the place that sustains their ancestral sense of self, the place they return to—at Easter, on saints' days, for memorials and celebrations—to keep traditions, and a link to the past, alive.

But place also pertains to the relationships we foster with the wider world around us. "Awareness," says the writer Sigurd Olson, "is becoming acquainted with environment, no matter where one happens to be." One autumn, while putting the shopping in the bed of our truck, I watched a kestrel arrow low over the supermarket car park, snatch a small mammal from an abandoned lot piled high with rubble and debris, and settle on a hummock of broken concrete beneath a streetlamp to feed. It was so close that I could make out the black fretwork on its cinnamon back, and our eyes locked together when its head suddenly swiveled. Shoppers pushed their trolleys past me, and I could hear the slam of closing doors, but I was so caught up in the eyes of the kestrel that I just stood there with a bag dangling from my hand. I watched with wonder until the very moment it left.

It's difficult to define place with any precision, as each of us comes at it from a unique angle. It can be suggestive of anything from a bricks-and-mortar home or neighborhood to an exotic and distant land. For some it might be wilderness, while for others it's civilization. It could equally be a meeting ground of the two. In fact it's hard to define place at all, let alone precisely. And that's what makes it so inviting—its rough edges and overlooked shades, the so-close-to-home that it's easily missed.

The car park and adjacent lot looked like nothing at all that day, but then nothing is what I'd expected of them. Perhaps that is the very essence, and beauty, of place, even if I can't define it. The way anywhere can take hold, and burrow deep within. The way it can dance when we allow it to. Which is why these days I prefer to think of *place* as wherever I happen to be, and the relationship that can be brokered with it.

More than a decade ago my partner, Julia, and I left London to move to a mountain village beside the Prespa Lakes in the southern Balkans. It's been a remarkable experience on many levels. The lake basin supports an astonishing range of wildlife and a diversity of landscapes, from the two lakes themselves to the high surrounding mountains. In between are beech, oak, and juniper forests, alpine meadows and dense reed beds, as well as the three countries that come together around the water—Greece, Albania, and the former Yugoslav Republic of Macedonia. But over the course of many seasons I've become increasingly drawn to what is simple and close to hand, as well as farther afield. I've learned that I don't necessarily have to cross the borders, or travel down the valley to the lakes, to meet with wonder and fascination, though I continue to make those journeys with as much interest as ever. Instead, I've learned that if I'm looking carefully and openly, with all my attention focused on that moment, on the small things that might surface in a given space, that I don't have to go very far at all. Sitting on the porch on a spring morning, when the sun strikes a mineral seam in the stone wall or a beetle bends a flower stem, can be an equal experience.

At the heart of this book is a belief best articulated by the artist Alan Gussow: "The catalyst that converts any physical location—any environment if you will—into a place, is the process of experiencing deeply. A place is a piece of a whole environment that has been claimed by feelings. Viewed simply as a life-support system, the earth is an environment. Viewed as a resource that sustains our humanity, the earth is a collection of places." We are continually capable of deepening that acquaintance, of becoming intimate with more than one place, of being at home wherever we find ourselves. In an age when the ecological integrity of our planet is threatened on so many levels, anything that strengthens those connections, or makes meaningful our daily arrangement with the world around us, is a form of resistance, a kind of love forged with home that has the potential to be fiercely protective.

I wrote this book at the edge of three countries, in a place that has changed me in immeasurable ways. But I would like to think that a similar book could have been written somewhere else, where it would, of necessity, have taken a different form, adopted a shape more in keeping with the local terrain, been influenced and sustained by the unique people, landscapes, and wild creatures it was inspired by. It would be colored by a different light. But at the small heart of it, in whatever part of the beckoning world it was set, would be our capacity to see things anew.

Shadow Grounds

IT WAS THAT TIME AGAIN; each year it occurred as an unexpected grace note, a sudden flourish to accompany the slow fading of summer, like the lifting of haze from the lake, the leaving of birds. Increasingly, though, it was a quieter affair, signaled by the heaving chorus of fewer and fewer animals. The Sarakatsani were on the move again, bound for their winter quarters, and they were taking with them the cows, goats, and sheep that constitute their livelihood. The fully loaded trucks and trailers had wound their way down the frosted mountain valley early that morning and were now paused in our village square: there were last goodbyes to be said, wishes for a safe winter to be offered, coffees to be bought for the road. While some of the drivers mingled around their trucks, smoking cigarettes or checking oil levels and brake lines, the deep moans and tremulous lowing of the animals rose and fell like a collective breath. The warmth of their jostling bodies materialized through the slatted sides of the trailers as a thin film of cloud. The air was rife with the reek of herds.

The Sarakatsani are transhumant shepherds, pastoralists who move with the turning of the seasons, journeying back and forth with their animals between summer and winter grounds. Traditionally they wintered their large flocks on the plains and coastal flats of central or southern Greece and migrated on foot to reach summer pastures in the mountains of the north, but the earthy tumult of those marching herds was replaced long ago by the convenience of trucks. Many of these vehicles have since been silenced as well, as the Sarakatsani become increasingly settled in their lowland villages. Despite this, a few small communities can still be found on the high summer meadows, continuing their centuries-old custom of calling two places home.

☼

I have often wondered about the nature of home, having been born in the northeast of England when my parents were in the process of emigrating to Canada. As a result, I spent the first few years of my life seesawing between our native port town and the north shore of Lake Ontario, while they searched for work and a place of possibilities. Eventually they settled near Toronto, where I grew up and went to school, comfortable with that placid, suburban landscape. Soon after finishing university, however, I felt an overwhelming urge to return, to go back to the country of my birth. It was a land I was familiar with from the accents and recollections of my parents and their transplanted friends, through brief summer holidays and the doting attention of relatives. But in the end I was drawn back by something incalculably smaller and more difficult to define: the resonance of place.

Certain places follow us, like shadows. At times they lengthen and stretch implausibly tall until they tower above our lives, or slant decisively away, as if trying to flee. Occasionally they appear not to be there at all—so exact is the overlay of self and place, so precise the meridian sun. Whether seen or not they are undoubtedly close, tethered by subtle threads spooling us forever back, either in memory or actuality, even dreams, to landscapes that articulate something of our selves.

We were on holiday in the north of England when I first glimpsed what would become my own shadowing landscape. A flat gray sky sheeted above the mysterious, treeless moors as we drove a narrow road in North Yorkshire. On either side of us the heather unrolled like bolts of rough, dark cloth, its dull purple flowers scattered like a fall of ripened berries. I remember the pockets of spectral mist that dissolved the second they were seen; the solitary, wind-stooped shrubs; the beautifully forlorn light. I was almost twelve that summer, and while I stared through the windows transfixed, the land began tilting me away from the enclosed space of the car toward a different kind of interior: luminous, revelatory, confiding. As I watched the ghostly moorland dimple away into nothingness, eventually merging with the solemn proclamation of sky, I became aware of a close and immediate attachment, a need to return. The place had been sealed like a secret in an undisclosed part of me.

I lived on the moors for a short, but emotionally rich, period of time. Although in the end I left them, I think and dream of them often, and they sustain me still. Instead, Julia and I made another home, in a village in the mountains of northern Greece. One summer, in the early years of living here, a friend and I set off at dawn to climb among those mountains. We used the river as our guide, winding between boulders and beech. By early morning we had edged beyond the tree line and were walking over pale tussocky meadows that sloped sharply toward the rising sun. As we rounded a fold in the high grassy hills, I pointed out the Sarakatsani encampment. We stopped to admire it, a rare and unlikely bloom. The hamlet comprised seven or eight thatched huts set in a mountainside scrape as neatly as inlaid stones. The elegant summer dwellings had been fashioned from tall reeds hauled up from the fringes of the Prespa Lakes, and each wicker dome was encircled by an earthen yard marked out by the braiding of thin branches.

While we stood there, a man and woman stepped out of their beehive home and began waving us over. Before we could even introduce ourselves we'd been seated at a rough wooden table in their yard, unexpected guests at a mountain breakfast. Antonia brought a plate of tomatoes to the table, followed by cucumbers, olives, and creamy slices of her handmade sheep's cheese. It hadn't been pasteurized yet and still carried the wild, musky tang of the hills in its taste. Giorgos brought a clear plastic bottle of fiery, grape-distilled raki and poured each of us a glass. He then withdrew an unopened pack of cigarettes from the pocket of his shirt; I watched him strip its cellophane and crumple off the foil, then tease out a single cigarette so that it poked obligingly above the others when he ceremoniously laid the packet before us on the table.

We tend to equate shepherding with rootlessness, the absence of a home. But what struck me as we sat together that morning was the realization that Giorgos and Antonia weren't passing through. Despite the seasonal nature of their dwellings, they had welcomed us with the same meticulous ritual and gracious hospitality that characterize many Balkan houses. The entire mountainside was their hearth.

Our hosts were probably in their mid to late fifties, and had been grazing their flocks on these same summer slopes for as long as they could remember. Twice a year they set out to cross half a country in concert with the seasons—both directions bringing them closer to home. They said their hearts belonged to the mountains, though, even if the encampment was little more than a reminder. A decade earlier and there had been as many as sixty or seventy people spending the season here; on feast nights, musicians played the Sarakatsani songs until dawn, while their kinfolk danced beneath an umbrella of bright stars. I looked around in the drenching daylight, wondering how far the raw wails of their clarinets would travel in the measureless, mountain dark. As elegant as a simple weave, I saw that home is a concordance with place.

"Unfortunately, there aren't enough of us to celebrate now," said Antonia.

"What about your children?" I asked. They both looked at me and smiled.

"Young people want other things," said Giorgos, matter-of-factly. "Our son is studying political science at the London School of Economics."

We raised toasts to each other's health and laughed at the strangeness of things.

Some of the Sarakatsani returned in the following years, but I didn't see Giorgos and Antonia again. Each autumn the shepherds brought fewer animals down off the high surrounding slopes, and the village square became a quieter place. As we'd sat there that morning beneath a pitched summer sun, sharing breakfast and listening to the distant meadow bells of the herds, a way of life was being whittled into memory. A few months further on, with the first frosts glittering across the hills, our hosts would have loaded their animals into trucks, closed the reed house we had sat outside of, and set off down the valley. As they journeyed south that day over the lowland plains, the spirit of the mountains would have stayed quietly close, shadowing them home.

Homing

THE HOUSE FEELS LIKE ICE when I wake. Julia is still asleep, so I stick to ritual and make tea before lighting the woodstove. Waiting for the water to boil, I open the curtains onto a frosted world. Snow has hugged the village overnight, replacing the lavender and thyme with smooth white hillocks in the garden. The limbs of the peach and quince trees are ridged in white, and the dried sunflower heads wear hats of snow. The willows along the river loosen a mist with each brush of wind.

The garden is far from still despite the cold and snow. Great tits hammer against the branches of the peach, cracking open their finds. The birds are a blur, relaying back and forth to the sunflowers where they pull seeds like teeth from their sockets. The cherry-red clown faces of the European goldfinches nod above a stand of dried flower stalks, their wings sawing black and yellow bands through the iced morning. Sparrows are busy beneath the sunflowers, scouring the midden of husks and chaff for spilt seed, and a few starlings shake snow off the telephone wires. It lowers like a curtain through the air.

In winter I see these birds most mornings, in varying combinations. On any given day some species might be missing, while others will have taken their place. I might wake to find blue tits looking for insects in the quince, a wren rooting through the woodpile, or blackbirds skulking about the shrubs. But what unites these birds, beyond their tendency to mingle in winter, is how widespread and common they are throughout Europe;

they're comfortable in a range of landscapes and habitats, having reached a positive accommodation with disparate and unrelated places.

I first got to know these birds in London, where they're as content to inhabit the city's parks and streets and gardens as they are this stone village straddling a Greek valley. Before we'd arrived here, having cast off our urban life to try and make a home beside the Prespa Lakes, I would never have known how easily these garden birds are able to adapt to varying habitats. Watching them has been a lesson in integration. Home for these particular species is dependent upon an acceptance of differing conditions, an equanimity of approach. They are adept at acclimatizing to the environmental vicissitudes of place.

But home is also an idea, a complicated human construct often built over unstable foundations. It's an idea informed by intricate cultural traditions, frequently contingent on coincidence and unforeseen circumstances; it's at the mercy of whims and fancies, prone to reordered priorities as we age and change. As if these obstacles weren't enough, home is also a peculiarly personal realm; there's no size or shape that fits all, and nothing to say that a single one will be sufficient for the duration of our days. But the instinct to home is widespread all the same, even when the response is to keep moving, to never stay in one place. While being at home suggests a settling-down, a physical presence in a given location, it also concerns *being at home*, settled and at ease with one's ways and surroundings, even if that entails being continually on the move. The varieties of home are many, as profoundly unique as the beings that seek and create them. Its forms are a testament to diversity.

In a whirl of movement, the garden birds are all gone. I never know what scares them up, whether they're unsettled by a car that's revved against the cold or if they sense my presence through the frosted window. Maybe a sparrowhawk curled in on the wind. Whatever it is that alarms them, they share the disturbance, rising in unison with a brief churring of wings. I step out while they're away to fetch wood for the stove. Snow dust glitters in the air, and the leaves of the sunflower stalks crackle with cold.

✵

Our part of London was rich, though not economically. It was the urban equivalent of a tidal zone: a place of plurality, of mixing and mingling. Drab 1960s estates had put down roots next to elegant Victorian homes. Young media professionals shared the streets with bewildered new immigrants from Bosnia and Kosovo. Second- and third-generation British Caribbeans drank in the Irish pub alongside overseas students and the unemployed. Variety was a virtue of the neighborhood.

Across the road from our apartment ran a row of local shops. Indian by origin, Ashwin sold newspapers, cigarettes, and soft drinks with a kindly melancholia, mildly perplexed when his children chose computer programming over inheriting the business. A couple of doors down were the Iqbal family. Having emigrated from Pakistan, they'd managed to squeeze enough food into the small grocery store to outlast a natural disaster. Recently arrived Iranians opened a pizza place, where each member of the extended family—from smiling teenagers to gracious grandparents—was engaged in some attentive aspect of the food's preparation. The Turks at the fish-and-chip shop had mastered and surpassed the craft of the traditional British dish and were neighbors with the Greeks running the late-night café, their historic animosity never hampering their hospitable coexistence. It was classic inner-city terrain, where the wealth of world cultures was well represented.

Few people stood out in this rich urban mix, but birds occasionally did. Common species like the goldfinch, great tit, and house sparrow were barely noticed, having been absorbed into the city's designs, but the rose-ringed parakeet lent a tropical touch, a dab of unexpected color, to the streets of London. The parakeet's emerald feathers are set off by a fire-engine-red beak and matching eyes. Its tail is as long as its body, and tapers to an impeccably fine point, streaked with blue above and splashed yellow below. The male gets to wear the rose ring of its name, looped loosely around its neck.

The rose-ringed parakeet is abundant on the Indian subcontinent, where it feeds in noisy numbers on agricultural fields and swarms in vast, twilight flocks to roost in the city trees of its native home. Now naturalized in Britain, predominantly in and around London, parakeets were first sighted regularly in the 1960s, and the circulating tales of their arrival are as colorful as their plumage. One account maintains that the first parakeets in Britain escaped from the set of *The African Queen*, filmed with Humphrey Bogart and Katharine Hepburn on a West London set in 1951. Another is premised on parts of a plane's undercarriage falling from the sky and damaging a tropical aviary. Finally, and with possibly the most enduring appeal, there's the story of Jimi Hendrix releasing a pair of parakeets in Carnaby Street, the heart of 1960s swinging London, as symbols of peace.

Most likely the first birds were feral escapees from private collections, but regardless of their origins they've adapted staggeringly well to London life. Being used to the monsoon rains of their native South Asian range, they've had little problem contending with the wet, North Atlantic climate. And the profusion of berries, nuts, and seeds growing in London's numerous royal parks and suburban gardens has left them little difficulty procuring food.

While we lived there, a spectacle unfolded each evening on the outskirts of the city that revealed the extent of the parakeets' successful adaptation. Many of the region's parakeets had chosen as their roost the grounds of the Esher Rugby Club, where they spent the nights in the tall, surrounding poplars. As the roost became increasingly well known, the women's rugby team borrowed the bird's name and had it emblazoned on the players' bright green shirts. It was an honor justified by the dusk display, when seven thousand emerald birds flew in from all directions, noisily assembling in what may well have been the largest parakeet roost in Europe.

Our neighborhood seemed to support only a single parakeet, a creature that put in fleeting and mysterious appearances; we never knew when to expect its solitary flight. Each time we heard its wild and raucous squawk we lifted our eyes, hoping to catch the emerald streak as it sparked through the sky. It seemed more like a shooting star than a bird, briefly materializing in the drenching rain as we walked to the Underground station, or flashing past Ashwin's shop as we emerged with the morning papers. It would slip into our orbit for a few seconds, hypnotic as a dream, before extinguishing beyond the rooftops.

Over the years, a friend and I often talked of making the journey to the Rugby Club roost; we pinpointed its location on a map and worked out the best way of approaching it by public transport. Whenever we snatched a skyward glimpse of brilliant green coursing between the buildings of our neighborhood we mentioned it again, but we never made it. I think we both secretly harbored a loyalty and attachment to our local parakeet. The easy joy of viewing a roost seemed like betrayal; the parakeet in our midst had chosen to home in the same place as us.

During our last year in London, I worked near Brick Lane, one of the city's most fascinating and difficult-to-define avenues in an East End already richly layered with shifting and vibrant histories. At the heart of London's Bangladeshi community, Brick Lane is dotted with curry houses, both upscale and everyday. Grocers lay out gardens of fruit and vegetables unknown to most in the country and shops sell bright swathes of patterned saris. Artists work from lofts in the side streets, while working-class pubs and cafés have retained their traditions and continued to resist the expanding gentrification of the city. But this particular design, this specific arrangement between cultures and place, is only the most recent reincarnation of an area that has witnessed myriad people laying claim to it as home.

As far back as the seventeenth century, Brick Lane was a safe haven for Huguenot refugees from France, Protestants violently persecuted and exiled for their faith in an overwhelmingly Roman Catholic country. In the wake of the Huguenots came Irish weavers displaced by dire economic conditions, who transferred their skills to workshops dotted around the area. But when the Russian Empire exploded with violent ethnic pogroms in the late nineteenth and early twentieth centuries, these same streets became home to an exodus of Ashkenazi Jews who founded weaving and tailoring shops. Many in the Jewish community eventually used their increasing prosperity to move out to the suburbs, and Brick Lane was subsequently resettled by Bangladeshis who had made the long journey in search of a new life.

A single building encapsulates the story of this shifting social habitat. The elegantly imposing edifice still standing on the corner of Brick Lane and Fournier Street was built in 1742 as a Huguenot chapel called La Neuve Eglise. By 1809 it had been renamed the Jew's Chapel, a place to promote Christianity amongst the expanding Jewish population of the East End. Only a decade later it would become a Methodist chapel, which it remained until 1898 when, in response to the large influx of Jewish refugees escaping the pogroms of the Russian Empire, it was consecrated as the Machzike Hadass, or Spitalfields Great Synagogue. By 1976, when most of the Jewish population of the area had left for the suburbs, the original Huguenot chapel became a Muslim place of worship, and was renamed the Jamme Masjid by the Bangladeshi community.

When the mosque was first conceived as a chapel, the Huguenots had a sundial set into the exterior wall between two arched windows, and its Latin inscription, *Umbra sumus*, unknowingly foretold the following two and a half centuries of its history. *We are shadows*, it says, divining the successive waves of East End arrivals that would sculpt the building's identity in accordance with their temporary needs. Weightless and shifting though we may be, the notion of homing remains a central and essential theme in many lives—a desire to root that recurs.

Despite the rich cultural diversity and moments of bright beauty, London was taking its toll on us personally. Having bookended the day with long commutes across the city, we had little time or energy left to enjoy its pleasures. Instead, we experienced the strange disquiet of a change beginning within. It revealed itself through arising concerns, through longings that suddenly loomed, large and unexpected, in our lives: the impossibility of silence in the city; a craving for wild spaces to live amidst; a wish to grow our own food and engage more deeply with the natural world; a need to make time for our passions and interests.

Along with the desires inching us in a new direction came the inevitable drift from the place where we lived. By whatever mysterious process that one makes a home, the reverse is equally unclear. But through the same inner reckoning that told us to slow things down, to find a rhythm more in keeping with the circling of the seasons and the heart's steady measure, we knew we could no longer make the accommodations necessary for our relationship with London to work. They struck us more and more as compromise.

For many of us, there comes a time when we set off for home. The journey might span innumerable countries and take up the best part of our lives, or it could equally mean accepting the way things are. But whether our particular notion of home sparks a long and uncertain search for a place to belong to, a family that makes us whole, or a spiritual yearning for equilibrium, we pursue the idea, or feel its lack, with an ache that trumps most others. Julia and I had reached an unforeseen crossroads, and we didn't know which way to turn.

※

Between the pigeon and the peregrine exists a world of urban birds. Whether regular or rare, they are at home in the city, and what sustains them is adaptation. Descending from the Latin *adaptare*, meaning to fit or make suitable, *adaptation* refers to a process of accommodation, a coming to terms with one's environment, a series of adjustments continually refined.

Some species are more able to fit in than others. They have a greater capacity for environmental variations, an ability to adjust to fluctuations and change, to make the most of opportunities. Back in the heyday of home milk delivery in Britain, the blue tit somehow became aware that beneath the foil cap of the glass bottles standing on doorsteps was a layer of energy-rich cream, there for the taking. By perching on the rim of the bottle, the birds learned to peck through the foil and sip out the cream. Some even tore the whole cap off.

But two things brought about the eventual demise of this urban adaptation. First were the fading fortunes of the milkman. As people embraced supermarket shopping more and more enthusiastically, the days of home milk delivery were numbered. Ultimately, however, this change in consumer habits would prove irrelevant to the birds, as it turns out that blue tits are unable to digest milk, only the fat-rich cream that rises to the surface. Along with the general shift toward supermarkets, shoppers were becoming more health conscious as well, and the popularity of full-fat milk fell dramatically in favor of skimmed and semi-skimmed milk, so that the few bottles still home delivered were indigestible to the birds.

Unlike the blue tit, which has a long history of living in cities, the black redstart is a recent urban arrival. A small, ashy-black bird with a rust-red fan for a tail, it likes singing from a high, prominent perch, and its song includes a memorable, crunching line once described to me as sounding like someone walking on gravel. Traditionally, the black redstart kept to the mountains of central and southern Europe, a native of stony upland slopes and scree, boulder-strewn ravines and steep cliffs. But its range expanded across parts of lowland Europe when it discovered aspects of the human-built environment that were similar to its own, adapting to church towers, industrial chimneys, and rundown factories, where it utilized the high vertical features and brick or rubble surrounds.

Although a few isolated pairs had crossed the English Channel and attempted breeding in southeastern England in the 1920s and 1930s, the birds' breakthrough didn't come until the Second World War. From September 1940 until May 1941, the German Luftwaffe relentlessly bombed London in the Blitz. At the start of the campaign, the capital was targeted for fifty-seven consecutive nights. In that time alone, thirteen thousand tons of high explosive and more than a million incendiary bombs were dropped on the city. Tens of thousands of people lost their lives in the Blitz, hundreds of thousands were evacuated to the countryside, and over a million homes destroyed or damaged. Whole areas of London lay in ruins: great mounds of smoking rubble appeared overnight; roads suddenly terminated in moonlike craters where the hulls of collapsed houses teetered on the rim. But a curious thing began happening at these sites of ashes and stone, these places of incalculable loss. Londoners began noticing a small, ashy-black bird in increasing numbers, seeing the flare of its red tail across the city. Breeding in the stony cavities of the ruins, the black redstart had found a semblance of its native home, and as its population rose it became known fondly throughout London as the bombsite bird.

When at the end of the war the slow process of rebuilding began, the black redstart was pushed out again. Instead, it found favor with the dilapidated peripheries. As Mark Cocker writes in *Birds Britannica*, the bird adapted to a range of abandoned or industrial areas, including "gasworks, sewage farms, railway sidings, marshalling yards, warehouses, timber depots, aggregate and scrap-metal works and industrial waste ground." But the current status of the black redstart in England is sadly precarious; only about a hundred pairs now nest in the entire country. They've succumbed to gentrification and development, losing derelict habitat to urban regeneration and the mania for tidying up London for the Olympics. It seems a home has been lost in the effort to spruce up the city.

Some years ago a friend was cycling along Brick Lane when he heard the unmistakable sound of someone walking over gravel. He heard it again, and then again, easily decipherable above the noises of the street, over the traffic rolling past and the clamor of commerce. Stopping at the edge of the road, he searched the walls and roofs on either side of him until he found the black redstart clinging to the lip of a soot-colored building and calling unconcernedly through the air. Few black redstarts can still be found so close to central London, but then the streets around Brick Lane have long been a place of refuge. Over time they've harbored many who have been seeking a new home. It's an area intricately layered in adaptations.

At times we need to turn away from a place when it no longer suits or sustains us, when our ability to adapt to its vagaries has run its course. This can be as true for other creatures as it is for us. Habitat, like home, is a fragile thing; it concerns a set of relationships torn easily apart. A shift in an ecosystem's qualities can tip the balance with the organisms it supports. But while some species might be lost, the changes may prove to be an inducement to others. This is not to suggest that habitat loss, the wholesale and willful eradication of natural landscapes, isn't responsible for both a diminished biodiversity and an increasingly impoverished world, but that within certain contexts habitat can signify many things.

Some of our most cherished landscapes are the direct result of human activity. When I consider the wild and treeless moors that ripple along the spine of England, shouldering out around the lochs and glens of Scotland, I think immediately of plovers and ring ouzels nesting among the purple heather tufts. I think of the curlew's haunted cry rising through the mist, of merlins and harriers carving open the skies. But the moorlands were once dense forest, emptied out for firewood and agricultural clearings from the Stone Age on. They are a relatively recent retooling of the land, one that has enabled a rare and sensitive habitat to arise out of its dark, peaty soils.

Despite being less obviously aesthetic than human-altered landscapes such as moorland, derelict urban and industrial areas like those favored by the black redstart can nevertheless provide rich possibilities for wildlife. A city's land is generally graded according to its economic and social utility, categorized as commercial, housing stock, or recreational. Where the land is seen as abandoned or unprofitable, released from its human measure, it is typically described as waste ground, a commonplace phrase founded on narrow and misleading terms. City spaces casually dismissed as vacant and empty are often full and vibrant with life; they can be both habitat and home.

Rephrased as *wild haven*, waste ground is a predominantly urban or industrial habitat that reflects nature's inestimable fecundity. Wildflowers and weeds quickly colonize disregarded land, free of pesticides and interference. Insects and invertebrates are attracted by the variety and abundance of vegetation, followed by birds and mammals, each enriching an ecosystem that for many is invisible at best. Mark Cocker describes these sites as "uncared for, unmanaged and unintentional." As a result, he suggests they are perhaps the "nearest thing to true wilderness that we possess." They may not be beautiful in the conventionally accepted sense, but a place teeming with life deserves its own definition, not ours.

Despite development, London still has its neglected and overlooked habitats: the places where the tenacious return. They might be abandoned train yards wild with insects and vines, the flower-filled lots of fallow industries, or rogue trees leafing alongside derelict docks. Webbed with largely forgotten corridors, the city retains remnant spaces that coexist with its contemporary designs. Canals that once carried a world of goods after they'd been unloaded along the Thames are still maintained for houseboats and pleasure barges, but others lay like quiet and murky backwaters, now home to herons and kingfishers, abandoned shopping carts and swans.

Cities can continually surprise our expectations. At the close of Barry Lopez's short story "Winter Herons" comes a remarkable moment, when a flock of great blue herons descends through a snowstorm to land near midnight on an avenue in New York. The unnamed central character is stilled by this startling appearance, transfixed by the birds' arrival: the herons had "landed as if on a prairie." While one of them pushes "its long bill into the white ground," the life of the city continues, oblivious, around them. Someone steps into a hotel through a revolving door; a taxi slows down until the protagonist shakes it off with his head. He is the only one connected to this striking and particular moment, an epiphany allied to awareness. When the birds lift as one from the avenue, they travel north for a few blocks before disappearing beyond the spread of urban light. The story insists that nature's mystery can be a part of the city, as well as the wilds. It reminds me of the black redstart calling unexpectedly above Brick Lane, an image that invokes lives entwined. I see a descendant of the London Blitz adapting to the same uncertain and changing habitat as the immigrants below. I imagine the city, in a finely balanced moment, as a shared space to home in.

The winter flock returns to the garden where a sharp wind kicks up skirts of snow. The assembly is smaller this time, and less conspicuous, but there's a bird I see more rarely amongst the others. It breeds on the high mountains surrounding the village, nesting in the stone cavities that riddle the slopes, and descends to the relative shelter of the valleys and plains in winter. The black redstart stands out on the stone wall. Its tail flickers with a moth-like vibration. And then it sweeps across the garden, a fan of flames trailing a swirl of smoke over the snow.

Along with the many things that home might be, it can prove to be curiously serendipitous as well. After months of not knowing where to go, we were led to this Greek village by a book. Having read a glowing review of it in a bird-watching magazine, we bought the book on the off-chance that we might someday visit the region it described. But it took only a single evening of leafing through its pages, reading passages aloud, and looking at the photographs to reach a decision of far greater import, aided by a bottle or two of wine. It was a book that revealed a visible love for a particular place, and it captivated us from the start. Our crossed roads had been unexpectedly resolved.

In *Prespa: A Story for Man and Nature*, Giorgos Catsadorakis writes an honest and evocative chronicle of an extraordinary place in the southern Balkans that, until then, neither of us had heard of. The Prespa Lakes, Great and Lesser, straddle the borders of Greece, Albania, and the former Yugoslav Republic of Macedonia, and are home to rare pelican colonies, mountain mammals, stone villages, and Byzantine monuments. We hoped to make something for ourselves there as well, and in our last London days I glimpsed the parakeet streaking emerald through the sun and rain with a degree of affinity; I sensed the thrilling possibilities inherent in making a new home.

I stand fixed to the window. The woodstove crackles and creaks behind me, and my mug of tea steams against the pale light. The garden flock of finches and tits, sparrows, and a black redstart, is scattered about the snow, and I'm aware of how at ease these birds appear to be wherever I find them. I've seen the same species throng the hills and forests, nesting in numbers behind crumbling factories or along shop-lined streets. I've heard their springtime songs shimmer from the willows at the edge of the lake, bubble up from a few dust-coated shrubs leafing beside a supermarket, ring bright across flower-soaked meadows and stark rubble tips. These birds bridge the rural and urban divide, as well as spanning our definitions of the aesthetic. They display a knack for adapting to place. Moving between disparate habitats with a grace that is both enviable and instructive, they are ultimately at home in the world. And that, I've come to learn, is no minor thing.

The Other Shore

SOME DAYS the other shore seems far away. It rises in the blue distance like a mirage until it eventually untangles from the haze, only there if you look long enough, staring across the lake as though seeking land in an empty sea. But other days don't ask patience of you, the kind of stillness to see things through. They open willingly, fortuitously, revealing unforeseen moments nested within, encounters that linger long after their closing.

It was a June afternoon, and as a friend and I neared the lake we'd heard a rustling about the reeds. We stopped to listen at the water's edge, sure it was a wild animal coursing through. The reed stems shifted and swayed with its steps, and we hushed as the crackling grew louder, closer, waiting for the creature to emerge into the open. But when the head of a man poked from the pale thicket, we quickly adopted a look that suggested we'd just been casually hanging about. A second man followed the first from the reeds, with another behind him. More men appeared at our side, all wearing shorts and knee-high rubber boots, and the kind of weathered tan earned solely by working hard hours outside.

After exchanging hasty smiles we all stared awkwardly at one another, with a measure of mutual curiosity. I could tell by their appearance that none of the men was from this side of the lake, and by the same token they understood that we weren't from these parts at all. They were as unaccustomed to finding people walking for pleasure among reed beds as we were to seeing them materialize from their watery depths. But a landscape at the edge of three countries, where secrets and suspicions provide a common tongue, can continually confound and surprise.

A pickup truck slowed on a sandy track beside us. Nodding in our general direction, the driver stepped down to nudge a small boat into the water and set off across the lake. While the men hung about, lighting cigarettes from a single shared pack and waiting, presumably, for the boat's return, I asked them where they came from, and they replied with the name of an ethnically Slavic village on the Albanian side of the basin. I'd been to the village of Pustec on the shore of Great Prespa Lake a few times, most memorably to attend a wedding, and at the mere mention of the groom's name the conversation ran wildly away. Our mutual wariness was broken like a spell. Despite the many conflicts and problems that have blighted the Balkans in recent memory, few places in the world are more hospitable. With a stranger's hand on your shoulder, or clasped firmly in your own, conversations can strike up in the oddest of spots; bonds that last years can be forged within minutes.

Like so many Albanians in Greece, the men were agricultural laborers, working for the man who'd gone to pull their dinner of fish from the water. Though they'd emerged from the reeds wearing waders, and some considerable distance from any farming fields, I decided against asking questions. Some stories are best left untold.

Instead, as we stood on the evening shore where the light lowered and broke like a mirror across the water, they were keen to know what I'd thought of the wedding in their village. The memories came easily back to me, lit by the vivid clarity of the absorbingly unfamiliar. That morning Julia and I had joined a convoy of old cars, polished and strung with ribbons, to collect the bride from a tower block where she lived with her parents at the edge of a nearby city. A trio of Roma musicians led dozens of us up the dark stairwell, the drum, clarinet, and accordion blaring Balkan songs that echoed throughout the building until each of us was hammering on the railing to their rhythms. Families stood on the lip of their apartment doors to watch in the dim light, some still dressed in slippers and nightclothes. I returned their smiles as we passed by.

Reaching the top floor, we squeezed into the bride's apartment, where bottles of raki, beer, and wine weighted each corner of the tables. No one could move in the tiny space, but the music still raced through the room, swirling out the open windows to join the city. You met whoever was next to you with a smile, though it would have been simpler to kiss. Through the forest of raised arms I glimpsed the two fathers tearing a ceremonial circle of bread, and then clasping the two halves together again, a mark of their daily lives being entwined from then on. And when the bride dressed in white edged from a shuttered room, the cheers and clamor of the crowd drowned out even the band.

For some minutes the men and I shared our memories of the occasion—how the groom's mother hurled bunches of basil high onto the roof of the house to welcome her daughter-in-law when we returned to Pustec; how the entire village danced the day to its end after a ceremony in a shoreline chapel. For the men beside me, of course, it was just an ordinary wedding, the expected expression of their cultural traditions, and one of many such celebrations they'd attended in their lives.

Moving on to the problems of Albania, we talked about the long days the men needed to labor in Greece to escape their country's chronic poverty. They asked me about London after I'd told them I used to live there. Having heard that well-paid jobs were easily found, they wanted to know the cost of living to expect if they could somehow make their way to the city. I gave the men a rough tally of costs, and their faces slackened in reply. I could see them considering the figures, wondering whether I was lying or if I'd simply made a mistake. Coming from a country where a laborer's day wages would barely buy you breakfast in London, the costs were as astonishing to them as the wedding was to me. Our perspectives are shaped by experience.

Some years before the wedding, Julia and I traveled to Pustec on our first visit to Albania. Having only just moved to Greece, we spoke little of our new language, and even less of the neighboring tongues, Albanian and Slavo-Macedonian. So in the time-honored tradition of strangers in foreign lands, we relied for communication on a few basic greetings and the extravagant use of our hands and faces. As is often the case in rarely visited places, the children of Pustec were shyly curious about the visitors to their village. They followed us in a group, laughing and giggling all the while, then sprinting ahead to linger at the edge of the track before falling in behind again. One boy singled us out, though, and walked quietly at our side. We tried stringing together a few words of Greek in the hope of sparking a conversation, but the boy shook his head at each attempt, replying with what we could only presume was Albanian or Slavic, or a combination of the two. So the three of us wandered his village in companionable silence, past chickens roaming the streets and donkeys tethered loosely and braying in the meadows, where domed hayricks studded the fields and women in brightly patterned head scarves hacked at weeds in narrow plots.

Reaching the shore, we stopped to look at the lake, peering across the summer-blue waters to the hazy mountain valley that had become our new home in Greece, a reversal of the view I was just getting to know. I still recall the clarity of the unfamiliar in that moment, the sense of intense engagement that surfaces in a new country, the strange and beautiful land that encircled us. All about us shimmered something of interest: the lives and light of the lake; the patchwork of fields; the languages out of reach to us.

The boy turned to us at the water's edge. "Perhaps you speak English?" he suddenly asked. The question was phrased faultlessly, spoken with a formal precision rarely heard even among native speakers.

"Yes, we speak English. But how did you learn it so well?"

"We study English at our school in the village."

The boy paused for a moment, arranging his next thought. "My favorite musician is Ricky Martin. Do you like his music?"

I can no longer remember how honest I was with my reply, but I occasionally think of the boy when I wander beside the lake, when I see the waters ripple and roll into the blue distance, the clear and glittering air. Some days the other shore doesn't seem so far away.

The Memory of Land and Water

IN FEBRUARY 2000, *the Prime Ministers of Albania, Greece, and the former Yugoslav Republic of Macedonia signed a joint declaration making the Prespa Lakes region the first transboundary park in the Balkan peninsula. The leaders pledged to "protect the unique ecological values" of the area while maintaining a "peaceful collaboration" between countries.*

Tracks: An Opening   PRESPA

Tracks are an ancient, magnetic language—pulling us in with possibility. The elusive poetry of a print, unlike the muscular certainty of a border line inked in an atlas, reveals details of a life being lived. A tracery of passing impressions, tracks can be as delicate as the brushstroke of a bird's wings, as bold as a hunting fox. They speak a mutable tongue, transforming from the moment they appear before finally vanishing, to be eventually overlaid by another script. But if you happen upon a set of tracks in their brief and fragile time, they can tell you things you never knew. They can take you places you've never been, and lend form to a fleeting world.

It was an April morning, the alders and willows greening steadily by the day, the first flush of wildflowers coloring the pale sand. We'd come to the lakeshore to look for terrapins, scouring its seasonal fringe of marsh and shallow pools for the secretive creatures. After finding a few meandering trails the previous evening, we'd returned in the morning to see if they'd been in motion at night.

Julia and I stood at the edge of the lake. While our feet were fixed firmly in one country, our eyes searched the other two. Close to our home, the beach unfurling along the southern shore of Great Prespa Lake belonged to Greece. But across the water, spanning the mountains to the north and the east, lay the former Yugoslav Republic (FYR) of Macedonia. And to our west rose the high peaks of Albania. The three countries come together in the middle of the lake; on a map of the area the dividing lines are strict, angular, and decisive. They make no allowance for the mobile lives of people and animals, for shifting water currents, for the ways of wind and wing.

Artificial borders often bear little relationship to Earth's natural systems. The Prespa basin consists of two lakes, a mountainous hinterland, dozens of villages, a small town, and three countries, but it remains a singular place. Though the political borders disrupt the integrity of the watershed, not everything comprehends these distinctions. Apple growing is the main agricultural enterprise on the side of the basin belonging to FYR of Macedonia. During storms, some of the fallen fruit is swept into Great Prespa Lake, where it travels, when the water currents and winds are right, to the shores of Greece. Immigrant apple trees now flower and fruit along parts of the Greek coast, the land having held on to the cargo of seeds, rooting the unregulated arrivals.

I soon found a new terrapin track ruffling the beach. It had paddled shoreward in the night, gently scooping sand out along the way, its pointed tail trailing like a rope behind a boat. The tracks of a European pond terrapin oscillate like gentle waves. At times they intersect with another's—two graceful, time-consuming meanders knotted together like vows. The tracery remains constant: while the gait of many animals can speed up or slow down according to circumstance, the terrapin's passage over sand is marked by meticulously spaced furrows. In water the reptile reveals an astonishing agility, diving and swimming at speed, but it is separated from its true element in spring, when it must cross onto land in search of potential mates or to lay eggs in a soft hollow.

Clambering over a ridge of sand, the tracks turned in a wide arc. I followed them with bowed head. The high, fluted notes of a common sandpiper broke the stillness from the shore. The trail kept a straight course until it unexpectedly met something else. Bridging the terrapin trail in the pale morning sand, and dwarfing its delicate path, were the prints of a large brown bear. They were fresh, as if the animal had just left. I let out a breath of deep surprise. Secrets and signs surround us, and the land retains a memory of what passes.

Way Marking   ALBANIA

The paths can turn up anywhere. Some are obvious and well used, where they follow the shore of the lakes or run parallel with a road. Others are more remote, switchbacking down steeply forested slopes, meandering over stone. Every so often a white ribbon is seen hanging from a branch beside the path. Unlike the phenomenon of tying memorial ribbons to a single tree, the dispersal of these bows serves a more practical purpose: to mark the land with a way.

Seen from above, the paths would resemble the many tributaries that feed a river. They crisscross the border between Greece and Albania, radiating out through the oak and beech forests. At their edges lie empty tins of sardines and luncheon meat, the cracked shells of sunflower seeds, torn and discarded clothing. Countless feet have grooved these corridors into place. The pathmakers cross illegally, risking capture and deportation by the Greek border police. But the ribbons continue to guide the many who come next.

Albania has experienced one of the strangest modern histories of any European state. Immediately over the Greek border you are met by imposing gray bunkers in the stony hillsides. Each of these concrete domes has a long rectangular eye for defenders to aim from, deepening the feeling of being watched at the crossing. The presence of the bunkers seems understandable at first, given the nature of borders, but as the road slips away from the checkpoint and winds through a gorge of red earth, traversing a wide agricultural plain rimmed by mountains, that certainty begins to fade. The bunkers are everywhere, like mushroom caps after an autumn rain. They lay in long rows through ripening maize, dotted in perplexing patterns between orchards and vineyards. They appear unexpectedly at road junctions, squatting beside fountains in village squares, inset into willow-lined riverbanks. About 750,000 bunkers of varying sizes populate a country of fewer than three million people. And they were all built on the orders of one man.

Enver Hoxha, also called the Great Teacher or Sole Force, ruled Albania with a fierce adherence to Stalinism from 1944 until his death in 1985. Hoxha was renowned for his paranoia and isolated state of mind, which coalesced in his belief of being invaded from all sides. He had the bunkers constructed to protect against such threats, intending them to be indestructible. When Hoxha asked his chief engineer if they would withstand a tank attack, the man was made to enter one and endure a shelling before his answer was accepted. The nation has no money, and little will, to remove the bunkers in light of Albania's serious economic and social concerns. A few of the larger ones have been converted into homes or coffee shops, and some pass muster for lovers' trysts. But the rest remain resolutely part of the land, indestructible reminders of the recent past.

Albanians often joke about the bunkers, mocking the country at their own expense, but their dark humor masks a solemn era. Enver Hoxha was as adept at engineering borders in peoples' minds as he was on the land. For the best part of his dictatorship he had the country sealed from the outside world. To "escape outside the state" was a crime of treason punishable by a maximum penalty of death. Booby traps were concealed along the line and a band of soil—cleared of grasses, weeds, and stones—was raked smooth each night so escaping footprints could be tracked. The secret police, the Sigurimi, kept close watch on citizens' lives, and their vast network of informers usually contained a few members of one's family, friends, and acquaintances. Hoxha even managed to alienate himself from the usually cozy Eastern bloc, breaking ties with Yugoslavia, the Soviet Union, and China, until the country's isolation was complete.

Against this backdrop of fear and segregation, the final collapse of the Communist state in 1992 resulted in social chaos and a critical political vacuum. A mass exodus swiftly followed, when suddenly it was no longer unthinkable to leave. The border no longer represented prison and death, and people embraced the opportunity to flee Europe's poorest country at the time and enter the outside world. While many Albanians emigrated farther afield, most ended up crossing to either Italy, for those living in the west, or Greece, for those in the east.

All along the mountainous frontier between Greece and Albania, paths have been worn into the earth from that time. People crossing the border from the Albanian side are neither secretive nor furtive; they do it openly, a necessary fact of life. The workers are easily noticed, walking roads and crossing fields with plastic grocery bags or cheap holdalls containing a few basic necessities. The migrants often wait until dark before striking out, carrying as little as possible in order to more easily avoid the border patrols guarding the other side. Skirting the abandoned bunkers, they watch for the white ribbons that mark the way, journeying from one country to the next, or, as a young Albanian worker once told me, "from nothing to something."

The two countries are mutually dependent, though acrimony clouds the issues. As a long-standing member of the European Union, and despite its current catastrophic economic troubles, Greece holds a unique position in the Balkan peninsula, attracting migrants from its poorer neighbors where unemployment is more profoundly entrenched. Albania relies on these remittances to support its crippled economy. While it rightfully complains about the poor treatment and accompanying racism often directed toward its citizens in Greece, these complaints conveniently shift the focus away from the Albanian state's chronic inability to employ its own. Populist belief in Greece, on the other hand, often embraces the traditional immigrant stereotype: whatever societal ills and crimes haunt the country are blamed inevitably on Albanians, despite statistics to the contrary. But two of Greece's major economic sectors—agriculture and construction—are as dependent upon cheap, and generally unregulated, Albanian labor as the laborers are on Greek wages. Without the immigrant workforce, both legal and illegal, these two sectors would struggle, and potentially collapse.

In a remote and thinly populated area like Greek Prespa, where the major economic activity is bean growing, the absence of Albanian workers would be disastrous.

It took me a while to work out the significance of the white ribbons. They would turn up on my walks through the woods, frayed and fluttering. But when I first met an Albanian family on a path, the connection struck home. The man carried a bag of food and clothes, while his wife cradled their child. They smiled and said hello in Greek as they passed by. I turned to watch them go, and when they slipped deeper into the spring forest, quickly disappearing from view, I understood the meaning of the white bows tied around trees.

The family could have been headed anywhere in the country, but they were probably walking to work in Prespa. The large-scale growing of beans is extremely labor intensive. The Prespa beans climb up wigwams of bamboo-like reeds trucked up from southern Greece. Each year the hundreds of thousands of canes are sharpened, staked, tied in, taken down, and stacked by hand—Albanian hand. At planting and harvesting time, the roads and rural tracks fill up with trucks and tractor trailers taking workers to the fields at sunrise and returning them at the close of day. From the first turning of the earth, until the laborers lay exhausted on the heaped sacks of harvested beans, it is a season of blistering work.

Many of the Albanian workers in Greek Prespa come from just the other side of the lakes. For a while we maintained a friendship by this irregular route. We'd met a young woman in one of the lakeshore Albanian villages, but the family had no phone for us to reach her. Her father, however, sometimes worked for a farming family in our village in Greece. Each time he came he brought with him a letter and some photographs from his daughter. Although we didn't speak any of the same languages as our friend's father, with a series of smiles and gestures we tried to convey something of our appreciation as he proudly passed the items on to us. When his work in our village was finished, we would hand him a letter and a few photos of our own to give to his daughter in return. I've often imagined the journey of those letters lacing the lands around the lakes together. They were carried along mountain paths at night, tucked protectively in a jacket pocket by a father returning home for the first time in weeks, guided through the darkness by white ribbons tied to trees.

Surfacing   GREECE

It was Coastal Clean-Up Day, and a local NGO had organized an event on the shore of Great Prespa Lake to mark the occasion. Julia and I joined a few dozen school students and some adult volunteers on a bright autumn morning, intending to tidy up a section of beach near the terrapin pools. The teenagers were walking along the dirt track in twos and threes, laughing and kicking stones ahead of them, taking pictures with their mobile phones.

When the bomb detonated along the shore, we all lapsed into silence. A deep, collapsing echo tacked back and forth between the mountains like the closing notes of thunder. From the far end of the coast a cloud of pewter smoke rose above the willows. The kids only missed a beat or two before falling back into step, resuming the rhythm of their conversation, the lightness of their age. But a few of the adults stayed rooted where they were, guessing at the sad origin of the explosion.

Between 1944 and 1949, Greece descended into a vicious era of communal violence. Toward the close of the Second World War, the resistance movements that had valiantly opposed Hitler's occupation hardened into their respective ideological positions. While the Communist partisans saw Greece's future in the establishment of a leftist state connected to the Eastern bloc, the pro-royalists, backed by the British and U.S. governments, wished to restore the exiled monarchy. The civil war still lies close to the surface of Greek society; it's a scar that has never truly healed. Once we attended a dinner party celebrating the completion and consecration of a small garden chapel. Before the food was even served, both sides of the long table—one aligned left, the other aligned right—erupted into open hostility. A rancorous dispute ensued, set off by the attendance of three elderly men who'd fought with the communists, each side as emotively absolute as the other. The priest swiftly drank his wine, consecrated the chapel with little ceremony, and left quietly without saying good-bye.

Beneath the animosity simmers a sobering toll. Despite varying figures, the general consensus is that around 158,000 died in the civil war, including civilians and soldiers on both sides. The numbers of displaced persons tallies considerably higher, and the conflict left entire villages deserted. Northern Greece witnessed some of the earliest uses of napalm, and the most heavily bombed mountainsides have never recovered.

After a few hours of cleaning the beach, dragging tired rope out of the reeds and pulling tin cans and bottles free from the sand, we heaped the whole load into our pickup truck and drove off to meet the municipal workers who would dispose of it. They told us what they knew—that the army had carried out a detonation of a civil war–era bomb found at the beach. Though "controlled," the explosion was still powerful enough to blow out the windows in a taverna a hundred meters away and tear the doors off its outside toilets. From where we stood we could see a small fishing boat slumped half underwater from the raised waves of the blast. The workers pointed out the bomb site at the edge of the lake, and we went down to the shore to have a look.

Prespa is littered with the ruins of the civil war. The final, fierce battles of the conflict took place nearby as the royalist soldiers pushed the remaining communist ranks into the last corner of Greece. While some partisans battled against the odds on remote mountaintops, the remainder, along with fleeing refugees, funneled north into Prespa. Machine-gun dugouts gouge the high hills. Stone bunkers lapse back into the land. A narrow gorge contains a cave that served as a communist field hospital, where wounded soldiers were transported after being rowed across the lake. On a dry, stony ridge scattered with ancient junipers exists an entire village of stone buildings. Strategically sited by the partisan forces, it overlooks the land bridge that divides the two lakes. Standing there amidst the silence of trees and fallen stone, I've often looked down over the lakes and villages and wondered what kind of place it might have been.

Greek Prespa was emptied by the civil war: almost no one remained here at its end. Some of the refugees were Communists who feared reprisals, while others were perceived to be sympathizers. Many were violently forced out by the partisans themselves—in the vain hope of ensuring the organization's continuity—and the rest fled as innocents for fear of the coming storm. Yugoslavia sealed its border, leaving Albania as the only route open. The people of Greek Prespa fled from the advancing royalist troops along the isthmus between the lakes while British and U.S. warplanes, on loan to the Greek government, strafed them from overhead. The planes jettisoned their bombs, attempting to sever the land bridge. Refugees pushed across the narrow strand, struggling to reach the Albanian frontier a few kilometers away. Those that made it fanned out and rebuilt their lives in other lands. In total, a few hundred thousand Greeks are believed to have left the country, one way or another, by the end of the war.

In our village I've met elderly men and women who fled along that route and eventually returned. Their journeys took them to Poland, Czechoslovakia, and Yugoslavia, among other places. One man, who returned to run the village distillery from a mud-brick hut at the back of his house, had lived for years in Tashkent, now in Uzbekistan but part of the Soviet Union back then. Another had studied classical piano at the Warsaw Conservatoire. Years later, when he came back to Prespa, he discovered with dismay that people had little interest in the classical repertoire. He picked up an accordion and began playing popular songs in tavernas and cafés instead. Most of the Prespa refugees never returned, though; they remain out there still, assimilated into myriad cultures. Their new lives were no easier to leave than their old ones.

We crossed the slanting beach to reach the bomb site. More precisely, we were walking on old lakebed tufted with tiny blue flowers. Though the exact causes remain unknown, the water level of Great Prespa Lake has dropped considerably over the last half century. Along with the loss, secrets are surfacing from an earlier age: live ordnance half buried in the mud. A great circle lay at the edge of the lake where the bomb had been. The sand walls were collapsing, caving in with a ripple of brown water. A few pelicans drifted toward a cove while egrets filled in the marsh like a fall of snow. Waves rapped the hull of the tilted boat. A strange silence accompanied the crater—the quiet, reflective aftermath of an empty devastation. Someone joked about the irony of it being Coastal Clean-Up Day.

A few days later the crater was gone. The waves had eroded its edges, the winds backfilling it with sand. But other bombs lurk in the lake mud; dusty grenades hidden in the debris of abandoned homes; live bullets wedged into the plowed earth, brought out briefly into the light before being turned back under. In spring, orange-tip butterflies drift along the marshy coast where the crater had been, drawn to the unfolding purple flowers of honesty that spread like a meadow along the shore. Though what has passed can no longer be easily traced, the butterflies enact its echoes. They home in on the flowering plants, the orange tips to their creamy wings like landing lights signaling their descent.

Rivers of Stone, Road of Grass   MACEDONIA

A whole glade of painted ladies appeared in the mountains above the lakes. We were walking with friends when we found them, midway through a daylong journey to a glacial lake hidden among the high peaks. Dozens and dozens of them flitted about our feet, adorned in black and orange with daubs of white near their wing tips. They roamed the sunshine from one frill of purple vetch to the next, and each flowering spray drooped heavily from the attention.

The painted lady is one of Europe's few long-distance migrant butterflies. It sets off from North Africa each spring, crossing the Mediterranean to spread throughout Europe, continuing to the tip of Scandinavia. It's hard to believe in such crossings: the thin powdered wings, fragile as tissue paper; the filament legs; the slender thorax buffeted by strong winds and storms. But this many, at least, had made it as far as a mountain meadow in FYR of Macedonia.

Wreathed in the hazy glow of the lakes, the alpine meadows were wild with the tendencies of spring. White asphodels sparkled in the sun, lark song showered from the sky, and the steady drone of awakening bees encircled us. But the grassy mountain slopes have hosted other things over time—namely thousands of soldiers during the First World War. They preserve some of them still. The mountain folds and sharp pinnacles of stone formed the western end of the Thessaloníki Front. On one side camped the Allies, composed mostly of French troops in this sector, but including British, Senegalese, and Nepalese soldiers, as well. German forces balanced the other side of the movable line.

A contemporary French newspaper published a map titled Sur Le Front de Macedoine. It shows the Prespa Lakes and their alpine hinterland heavily banded in black wavy lines that depict the shifting allied front. The first line curls along the southern edge of Lesser Prespa Lake and is dated September 30, 1916. The next black band runs along the isthmus that separates the bodies of water, about seven kilometers farther on. The date reads November 11, 1916. It took the allied forces forty-two days to gain the ground that takes a few pleasant hours to walk.

Midway between that second front and a third, drawn across the map as a slightly beveled line, we stumbled upon the meadow of painted ladies while making our way toward the lake nestled in the high peaks. But rather than the wildflowers and warm sun that welcomed us, along with the birdsong of arriving migrants, the French troops endured four months of an awful winter on these slopes. The conditions were so atrocious that G. Ward Price, reporting on the Macedonian campaign as the Allies' official war correspondent, described the hiatus as a "winter of enforced inactivity owing to mud." Even in summer the mountains can feel forbidding; they offer little cover and are exposed to raking winds that keep the meadow grass and isolated shrubs stunted and tough. When the French finally began to advance from their mountain position on March 11, 1917, with the aim of reclaiming the town of Resen at the northern end of Great Prespa Lake, it coincided with the worst snowstorm of the winter. After the laborious preparations of carting supplies up to the front line along "seventy miles of absolutely abominable surface," the troops were mired in a fierce alpine blizzard. Like myself, G. Ward Price surveyed the scene in a warmer season, a month or so after the initial assault. As he "toiled up those steep, rock-strewn mountains in dry weather it seemed impossible to believe that the French had been fighting there with the snow lying several feet thick."

The French army did more than just fight in these winter mountains, though; they also built a road. It was the same road we were walking on as it wound among the high cathedral peaks, carrying us closer to the glacial lake. I had asked about the route the evening before, while eating dinner in the village we'd stayed in. "Just follow the French road," had been the restaurant owner's reply nearly a century after its construction. Built to supply the front line, it had borne the weight of large-wheeled artillery, canon carriages, and horses pulling rations and ammunition. Walking its length, I saw how much of it has been reclaimed by the steep mountainsides from which it emerged. But that doesn't lessen the remarkable achievement of its engineering; it only alters the perspective.

Weather shapes its own designs. The same severe conditions that kept the allied forces pinned to the mountain massif also gave birth to the range's most extraordinary feature: its rivers of stone. Whole alpine folds are flood-washed with rocks, long spillways tumbling from the crests to the valleys far below. These rivers are the result of weathering, released by a process of continual freezing and thaw. When a stone loosens, it joins the torrent of great granite boulders that preceded it. Some of these stone rivers are more than two kilometers in length, and can be up to three hundred meters wide. During the winter of 1916, the French troops must have worked out a way to clear a path through these chutes of stone, as no mounted artillery or wheeled carriage could have forded them as they are today. They somehow dammed the rivers where the road was meant to go.

There is an ethereal beauty to what time, weather, and the wild do to man's inclinations. They embrace, soften, and fade them, and finally overtake them. Wherever the French road crossed a stone river it's been washed away, absorbed into the flow. The road is losing its hold, not as quickly as scripts in the sand, but just as surely. Grass grows over much of its course, and in places it's more like a path, where wild pansies and asphodels catch the swelling light, where painted ladies move amongst the flowers having crossed whole countries and a sea.

I can see the border with FYR of Macedonia from our garden in Greece. It runs along the top of a treeless ridge that Julia and I call Table Mountain. When seen from the high peaks that rise up behind it the ridge actually slopes quite sharply, but from the perspective of our home it is as flat as the wooden table where I write. But appearances are often misleading.

In the summer of 1917, G. Ward Price reported that "eighteen months of very great labor, much sickness and hard fighting . . . have left the Balkan campaign in a temporary condition of deadlock. As things stand at present the enemy's front and our own have proved mutually impregnable." Things aren't so very different today. Though the entire lake basin is visible from each of the three countries, those other shores are more distant than they seem. One border is marked by a series of white, stone obelisks, the country's name inscribed in the Greek alphabet on one side and in Cyrillic on the other. With the disintegration of Yugoslavia in 1991, the Republic of Macedonia claimed independence, but Greece doesn't acknowledge the country's constitutional name. Its own neighboring province is called Macedonia, and the dispute hinges on serious issues of historical identities, land claims, and cultural ownership.

A real bitterness hangs over the two countries' relations. There is no easy way through the complex conundrum, and views are hardening on both sides. But it means that natural systems like the Prespa Lakes will remain strictly divided for the foreseeable future. On the other side of the mountain border nestles a village similar to ours. Living there is a friend old enough to remember when the border wasn't impassable, a time before it was sealed as the Greek Civil War reached its terrible conclusion. He can recall traveling by horse and cart with his parents—from their village in one country to ours in another—to celebrate its saint's day festival. The distance between the two villages is only a few kilometers, an unremarkable measurement when laid next to a map of the painted ladies' migration, but the journey now takes about three and a half hours by car, a circuitous route through distant cities and strictly controlled border posts. While the old French road is slowly giving way to the wild, the front line between peoples has held.

The damp sand perfectly preserved the bear tracks. We'd scoured the same area the evening before, and other than the fine, delicate steps of a fox, we had found little else. The prints were deep and clear, each individual claw slicing sharply into the shore. Following the steps backwards, we traced the arrival of their course.

We hadn't wandered far before discovering that the tracks met up with a second set of impressions. Two adult bears had passed in the night, one marginally smaller than the other. Over the years we'd seen dozens of brown-bear tracks around Prespa, finding them deep in the beech and oak woods, sunk into autumn meadows or crusted snow. But there on the shore we'd stumbled upon a more unusual script, an enigma in the language of tracks. The tracks stopped in the same places, side by side at the edge of the lake, suggesting the bears were journeying together.

I could easily picture a single bear moving through a landscape, rambling in the anonymity of night. But finding two sets of trails demanded greater attention. The tracks asked questions instead of answering them. The European brown bear is essentially a solitary creature. Although there are times when two adults might be seen together—a brief mating period, siblings that don't separate—these occasions remain rare. We would need to cross a border of our own imagining, to perceive beyond the comfort of the easily summoned. The tracks articulated a relationship, not only with the land but each other.

Coming off the plateau of sand that banks the river, the bears walked single file at the very edge of the lake, their paws sinking cleanly with each step, until one moved out of the wake of the other and traveled by its side. Occasionally they stopped to face the lake. From the way their prints arched inward, settling more deeply and distinctly, they appeared to have stared over the dark waters for a while. Perhaps the reflected lights of far villages caught their curiosity.

One bear left the other to climb the sloping sand where it met the trail of the terrapin. Or perhaps the terrapin descended later and met the path of the bear. Wandering over the beach grasses, the bear turned in a sweeping arc over fine yellow daisies, closed up during the night but now opening with the morning warmth, toward the marsh. Separated by the long band of moonlit water, the terrapins' seasonal haven, the bears continued their journey.

As I followed the shoreline tracks I became aware of a different way of thinking. Walking in the steps of the bears brought me closer to their world. Something of my own solidity was suspended and I opened, however imperfectly, to another way of being. Did the bears call to each other from across the strand, or did they pad along in silence? What sounds alerted them to the nocturnal world? Where were they going? What relationship bound their passage? The prints retained the animals' presence, inviting us into their lives.

The bear nearest the shoreline suddenly sheered away from it. It entered the marsh instead, where the waves would have sloshed from end to end. The murky heave must have been heard along the shore by night creatures and roosting birds. The bear waded through the pond and then stepped heavily from it, water draining from its darkened fur while it fell in behind the other. The two animals continued their course for as far as we walked, until we lost their tracks in a tangle of marsh grass.

A bear's knowledge of borders is different from ours. It belongs to a *place*, to a suitable habitat and range, and remains persistent in playing its part in it. A bear's tracks, like the steady passage of a terrapin on sand, come and go; they are easily lost to water and wind. But they are less ephemeral than they might seem. While the monuments of man's great certainties are slowly reclaimed by time and the elements, the tracks endure through the simple act of repetition, reinscribing the land with their unwavering constancy.

Walking in the bears' steps tightened the weave of the Prespa basin, threaded the lakes and three countries together, transforming the term transboundary into something more than just a human designation. I imagined the bears descending from the high mountains through a glade of migrating butterflies. Clambering over stone rivers, they follow an old grassy road ground into place by artillery and troops, where soldiers lost their brief lives for a step or two of snow meadow. They carry on down to the coast, rubbing against rogue apple trees seeded by storms. Following the waterline, the bears pass a bomb crater reborn as a marsh, where terrapins arrive purposefully in spring, laboring over the sands to mate and lay eggs. The bears walk the narrowing isthmus—the land bridge for refugees running from warplanes strafing overhead—and then climb up into the starlit hills of limestone and wild thyme. They find a well-worn path among the oaks and junipers, where in the quiet stillness of the night they brush against frayed white ribbons knotted onto branches. Passing the wide-open eye of a long-blind bunker, the bears move off into darkness.

An Accumulation of Light

IT REACHED ME as an afterglow. We were walking on a cliff-edge path when a faint light glimmered at the corner of my eye. I stopped and looked down on the sea for a while, reluctantly accepting that it must have been the sparkling roll of a wave that I'd seen, a crest of bright water. I'd taken a few more steps along the path when I saw it again, fleetingly, like a vague memory dredged from the depths. Watching the water more closely this time, I looked for disruptions in its undulating rhythms. But nothing other than sunlight played on the vast surface of the Black Sea. From seventy meters up, at the top of red sandstone cliffs, the sea was spread out in a shimmering blue glaze, brimming with polished light after the early-morning storms. Whatever I'd seen had subsided, gone back to its secret depths.

I was turning to join the others again when I saw an unmistakable shudder close to shore, a rippled undertow of motion. And I was still holding my breath when the silver arch of a dolphin broke the surface and caught the sun on its flukes. I must have yelled out because suddenly people were around me, my friends pointing joyfully toward the waves, and a few French tourists asking what all the excitement was about. Another dolphin leapt clear of the water, then two of them in perfect synchronicity. They climbed into the air, passing with graceful ease from one medium to the next, dragging sprays of water like silver harnesses from their tandem tails. They seemed suspended in an enduring moment, balanced on a high wire slung above the sea. Water droplets sloped from their sides like shards of light.

About a dozen bottle-nosed dolphins made up the pod. They crested the surface of the sea with their beaks, playfully nudging the lid of their world, and occasionally scribing arcs in the air. I later realized how time had dissolved while we watched the dolphins. Past and future, and all the weight they carry, had folded into one clear, immeasurable moment. Everything else had fallen away, brushed off like a scattering of crumbs. I was aware of feeling an ineffable joy, and lightness of being. Eventually the dolphins moved farther out to sea, where we watched them breaching in the distance like a range of receding hills.

The day had begun without promise. We'd risen early to spend as much time as possible exploring Cape Kaliakra, but a storm had gathered while we ate breakfast on the veranda of the hotel. Clouds funneled in from the east, purple bruises swelling above the incandescent sea. The wind was cold, and racing in off the white-capped water. When the rain came it resembled a riot, quickly turning streets into riverbeds, and drumming on the rooftops until it fell heavily from the eaves.

Our friends sat writing postcards across from us as the rain gusted in beneath the canopy. Each year Julia and I join them for a week of traveling and bird watching, and we'd chosen Bulgaria in order to follow the spectacle of autumn migration along the Black Sea coast. The cape was the last stop of the week, the place we'd been most eagerly anticipating, though it seemed the drenching rains would waylay any possibility of exploring it at length.

Cape Kaliakra, or the Beautiful Headland, is an escarpment of coastal steppe, a wedge of earth riding two kilometers out into the Black Sea. It is the easternmost point of Bulgaria, a plateau stilted on high sandstone cliffs and richly layered in grasses, wild herbs, and a scattering of scrubby trees. As a protected nature reserve, it acts as a beacon and refuge for both migratory and resident wildlife.

By midmorning the rain had slackened off just enough for us to agree to give it a go. We were staying in a town about a dozen kilometers from the promontory tip and while driving out of it, climbing through torrents of brown water and washed-away stones that were collecting in unintended lakes, we could see little ahead of us through the curtains of cloud and rain. Nearing the cape the rain eased, and a few spears of pallid light lit the grasslands. The road was strangely dry, and the soil at the verge only damp. We had come out on the other side of the storm, slipped through the elements like light through an aperture.

☼

The epic tales of migration are well known. The arctic tern, which undertakes the longest journey of all, experiences the most daylight hours of any animal as it annually circumnavigates the globe from pole to pole. Monarch butterflies travel staggering distances in fragile, swirling masses to reach ancestral winter roosts they have never seen before. Salmon steer themselves through ocean fathoms to the singular spot in the river where they were spawned years earlier. Remarkable as they are, these journeys are only fragments of the immense narrative of seasonal movement.

As we explored the grasslands and copses of Kaliakra we began seeing some of the smaller, quieter, less heralded stories of passage that were scattered about the cape. Long streamers of gray herons, sometimes fifty in number, wavered above the cliffs or the rim of the sea. Tides of white wagtails flew past us toward their southern appointments, steadfastly rising and dipping through the air like needles stitching cloth. Red-footed falcons were lined up on telephone wires, waiting for whatever signal sent them on their way. And an empty ledge of coastal cliff would suddenly hold a handful of wheatears scrabbling about for insects amongst the grasses; they had touched down that very moment having safely crossed a stretch of the Black Sea. The journeys of migrating birds that had girdled the earth in my imagination became visible. The pathways and corridors I'd seen drawn on maps took on a fuller form, like sails raised over rigging. We were witnessing the brief pauses and humbling flypasts in the birds' ancestral routes:

Everything beckons us to perceive it,
murmurs at every turn . . .

Many years ago a friend quoted these words to me from a poem by Rainer
Maria Rilke. They were lines he had first heard when a photographer he
admired used them as the title for a book of images. For my friend and me,
these words began to illustrate a method of seeing. The art of perceiving
is more about reception than it is vision. We don't have to struggle to see
things, Rilke suggests, for they are already there, calling us. The difficulty
lies in unlearning our tendency toward indifference.

I have always taken Rilke's words as an exhortation to explore the often
unnoticed, to be aware of the possibilities in all that surrounds us; they
are an appeal to apprehend the world in its entirety. His words are an
invitation to openness, encouraging us to let in the wild and unpredictable,
the ordinary and overlooked, the fleeting and unexplained. He counsels us
to be held in awe by the seemingly insignificant. There is possibility in the
smallest of things, the most innocuous of moments. More mystery can be
found in a few moments spent in a stand of trembling reeds than a lifetime
passed in an unperceived world.

Owing to its enviable strategic position overlooking the Black Sea, the cape
has had a long human history. A fortified settlement was first constructed
on the headland by a Thracian tribe in the fourth century BC. Since then
the promontory has seen Romans, Byzantines, Slavs, and Ottomans using
and reusing the remnants of fortification in successive cycles of domin-
ion. The cape was eventually designated a nature reserve in 1941, and the
remaining ruins of a medieval fortress still stand, solemnly encircling a
small military installation.

At the edge of the cliffs, a few minutes' walk from where we watched the
dolphins, stands a memorial sculpture called *The Gate of the Forty Maidens*.
It was raised to commemorate the legend of forty young Bulgarian women
who, as the sole survivors of an Ottoman sacking of the town toward the
end of the fourteenth century, and in preference to being captured by the

invading soldiers, braided together their long tresses of hair and jumped from the cliffs into the Black Sea.

The sculpture resembles an obelisk, and is composed of three stone figures. I circled the memorial, looking up into the faces of the falling women. Two of them are vertically aligned, so that the hands of one reach up to touch the toes of the other, while the third woman has her back to them, and is tied by her hair midway between the other two. The women are naked, as symbolically pure in their leaving as when they entered the world at birth. We see them falling as one, faces cast down to the sea. It is hard to contemplate a decision of such magnitude without imagining fear. On this flat and isolated promontory they would have had little chance to flee a life no longer their own, one of certain servitude spent in the presence of invaders. With their children captured and their husbands dead, they jumped as one without recourse to a change of mind. It is difficult to stand at the edge of the steep red cliffs without wondering what the final thoughts of those women might have been as the sea rushed up to meet them. Was it a last, desperate leap into the light?

Hearing that a pair of eagle owls inhabited a rocky gorge on the plateau, we decided it was worth trying to see them hunting about the cliffs at dusk. First we explored the area in daylight, getting a feel for it before evening. The gorge began at the sea in a small cove where a few fishing boats were dragged up on to the beach and a handful of people swam in the shallows. Our friends couldn't be tempted into the late September water and so they left us, trousers rolled up to our knees, walking the crystalline edge of the Black Sea. We'd only been in the surf a few minutes when they called us over, hushing us to come quietly to the pool of water they were standing by.

A squacco heron crouched on a stone at the edge of the pool. It was water lit, absorbing the mirrored light until it glowed. The bird's back was draped in ochre and violet; its breast laced with lemon yellow that bloomed toward the emerald edges of its eyes. It seemed to be the reflected emblem of the day, a distilled essence of light. The green and black lance of its bill was steady, and its eyes unwavering. It appeared to be lost in a trance but was peering for fish in the shallows, as still as the reflecting water. One of us must have shifted our weight, because suddenly it unfolded the white flags of its wings and glided away.

From the sea end of the gorge, the valley squeezed itself between high bluffs. The ravine was flooded with reeds, straw-colored palings staked around pools of open water where the skeletons of dead poplars still stood. We drove up the valley and searched the arid cliff face for caves suitable for eagle owls. The lane slowly narrowed, cordoning us between reeds and brambles, the thorns squealing against the sides of the car.

A purple heron, one of Europe's rarer birds, appeared unexpectedly ahead of us, where it stood almost a meter high. Robed in brown and purple, it began a slow, patrician walk across the road, elegantly stepping out on the twin stilts of its legs. The heron stopped at a thin grassy verge and lowered its head as if listening. Knifing the blade of its bill toward the seemingly quiet earth, it drew up a rippling snake about a meter in length. With its head clamped in the heron's bill, the tail of the snake swung free, grazing the road until the heron stood on it, trying to control it with its foot. The snake was stretched taut, pinched between the bayonet bill and the long, clasping toes of its captor as the heron tried to maneuver it in such a way as to swallow it whole.

All creatures have hidden energies, compelling them toward life. This explosively instinctive force was suddenly uncorked after the snake somehow came loose from beneath the heron's foot and was swinging above the road again. The heron began walking with the snake dangling from its beak, but managed a few meters at most before the snake found the heron's whistle-thin neck with its tail, coiled itself once, and began crushing the bird's windpipe. The heron shuddered in shock, staggering about on its spindled legs until it dropped the snake from its bill. Although the snake was now completely free, it maintained a tight noose around the bird's neck, lagging it like a pipe, slowly and methodically choking it. The heron snapped its head and bill back, desperately trying to dislodge the snake, and then slumped face forward to the road, thrashing its wings into the asphalt.

The wingspan of a purple heron can reach a meter and a half in elegant flight; unable to lift toward the sky, the diminished creature began crawling across the road on its quivering wings, taking the spiraled snake with it in the last breaths of its life. The heron strained to take flight, but its flailing wings stayed pinned near the earth. Finally it managed to pull itself off the road, slumping into a patch of grass and weeds where it laid trembling and laboring for breath. The snake was moments away from crushing the last of the bird's life when it suddenly fell away from its neck and disappeared into the undergrowth. The heron faltered and wheezed as it staggered to its feet, and then took weakly to the air, a purple bruise being spirited away.

☼

The afternoon circled toward dusk, its last light suspended in an amber glow. I walked out over the tough grasses and flinty stone of the steppe, needing a few moments to be alone, to pause and reflect on the depths of the day. I wished to breathe deeply in that vast landscape awash in light and mystery. These days and places are affirmations; they approach the numinous. The beckoning steppe, and the creatures it harbored, was revealed as radiantly and assiduously as a moon passing out of eclipse. It was as if the spirit of the place had become visible, had for a brief creak of time taken material form. I stood and watched how the light fell, flaring the flatlands in a copper-edged glow, sending silver sparks skimming across the endless sea.

Somewhere in front of me a bird flew quickly over the land before losing itself in scrub grass. I hadn't recognized its call and was curious enough about its flight to begin walking in its general direction, hoping to see it before it took to the air again. I never discovered what the bird was; instead I found something else, close by my feet. Startled by the sound of scurrying, I looked down to see a tiny quail running past my boots and weaving in panic across the scrub. I must have been almost on top of it when it finally bolted, as quails are extremely reluctant to flee. They have a remarkably determined sense of poise, staying quiet and still, regardless of proximity, until danger has passed. For a quail to emerge from cover is a sign of its desperation; I had crossed the line of its reckoning.

The quail stopped abruptly some meters from me in the sparse and exposed land and pressed itself against a stump of thorny twigs. It moved as close as it could to these slim facsimiles of cover, trying to afford itself some meager protection, but it was almost entirely visible. We stared and watched each other silently, its wet black eyes never moving from mine. About the size of my hand, the quail was migrating south to Africa. If it survived being heavily shot at by hunters around the Mediterranean, it would spend the winter somewhere on the warm continent before retracing its journey in spring. I was conscious of a palpable vulnerability as it tried to conceal itself from me behind a few crooked sticks.

I looked away momentarily to see where the others were. When I turned back to the quail, I caught a glimpse of it scuttling into a patch of evergreen scrub. It had watched me closely and with a studious sensitivity, firmly rooted in its knowledge of place; the bird had waited for its chance and then taken it. The appearance of fragility was only part of its story. The four of us studied the spot where I had seen it vanish, but it had gone to ground. The quail was in there somewhere, poised again and vigilant, safe in its chosen refuge, like the bones of the forty women that lay scattered beneath dolphins at the bottom of the sea.

On seeing dolphins in the Aegean, the writer and explorer Patrick Leigh Fermor wrote: "Each leap into the air called forth a chorus of gasps, each plunge a sigh. These creatures bring a blessing with them. No day in which they have played a part is like other days."

Some days outlive others. They are lit differently in memory—as resplendently as the squacco heron at the edge of the pool or the dolphins glimmering at sea—and they are brushed with an intensity that seems to suspend the customary passage of time. This was such a day. I have come to see it wrapped like a chrysalis in light; a day that left me feeling closer to the world, connected in some intangible way to its rhythms. Perhaps, as Leigh Fermor suggests, the dolphins had brought the day a blessing. Watching them had reminded me to be more generous in my seeing, to be aware of small things, the rustles and faint shadows that accompany possibility, the murmurs at every turn.

From the moment we passed through the morning storm it felt as though we had crossed a threshold, where the world and its ways were illuminated by a different order of light, a luster of unusual depth and candor, warm and confiding. The cape seemed to be a liminal place, porous and translucent, a landscape of transformation. Even the name of the memorial sculpture, *The Gate of the Forty Maidens*, suggested an entrance and exit, a passageway from one realm to another. When I first saw the obelisk commemorating the women, I had tried imagining what their final thoughts might have been. Now, recollecting that day, I wonder if, as they fell with braided hair toward the sea, their brief pasts and foreshortened futures weren't absorbed into that singular descending moment, so that there was nothing but a bloom of light and the air rushing past.

※

The umber cliffs were riddled with holes and small caves, like the perforations of a sea sponge. The sheer cliff-face fell away to the reed beds and pools of water that lined the valley. It was ideal habitat for an eagle owl: an inaccessible nesting site that was close to the rich hunting grounds of the steppe. The bird is the largest of Europe's owls, with a wingspan that can reach 1.7 meters. Seen at the entrance to its cave it would stand about seventy centimeters high, powerful enough to hunt deer calves, its sunset eyes glowing deeply from beneath thick, tawny ear tufts.

We began our watch with the last of the true light. Three men with binoculars and telescopes stopped nearby, and the youngest of them walked over to us. They were Bulgarian ornithologists, he told us, and his companions came here every year to survey the birds of the cape. Each previous time they had been successful in seeing the eagle owls, but this year they had doubts. Our new acquaintance didn't elaborate their uncertainty; it was an instinct, born of familiarity, that told them the owls had vacated this site, and were nesting, hopefully, elsewhere.

We all stood about, waiting patiently for the light to fade. In the quietness I found myself thinking about the struggle between the heron and the snake that we'd watched on this same lane an hour or so earlier. It was a mood that still clung to me, as uneasily as wet clothes. We scanned the rugged cliffs and listened to the cracklings of birds in the reeds. The extraordinary, piercing cry of a water rail curdled up from the marsh and echoed throughout the chambered stone—an extravagant voice for such a shy and seemingly unremarkable bird.

The Bulgarians gave up the watch first, shrugging their shoulders in the ghost light while loading equipment into their car. They drove off, leaving us alone in the ravine as dusk settled around us like fog and the rustlings and clickings of the reed bed gradually thinned. We stayed another quarter of an hour, but the light above the ridge was leaving and with it the possibility of seeing an eagle owl as it emerged from its cave, even if one had been there.

We drove slowly out of the ravine in darkness, winding our way back up to the plateau. As we crossed the steppe, a brown hare appeared in the milky light pooled around the car. It stared back at us as we slowed, its eyes like twin moons. The hare vanished into wayside shrubs and we continued slowly, hushed with the possibility of other encounters in this hour of nocturnal waking. A nightjar, that shy midnight hawk, glanced off the glow of the headlights. It was seen in a brief photographic flash, like a negative branded on the black skin of the sky. Even in darkness the wondrous light of the day threaded its way in.

The car crawled cross-country as we peered through the windows into night. The military base in the ruins of the fortress lit the tip of the headland, a burning cresset in the dark expanse. Reaching a crossroads, we turned into the last stretch of road before leaving the cape. A faint ribbon of gray light remained where the sun had slipped beyond the horizon, and the dark silhouette of an eagle owl was etched upon it. The owl flew from the solitary tree toward the sea cliffs where it perhaps now nests, its muffled wings bearing it off in a silent glide, the earth dimming it like a cupped flame, until it was taken up by the dark.

Gifts

THE ANCIENTS named them the halcyon days, the irrepressible interlude. They arrive in the depths of winter like an unexpected friend, and for an unseasonable week or so a radiant warmth spills over the land. The hours swell with the prospects of spring, the luxurious light notching smiles on the most reluctant of faces. The days then slip out like a wistful sigh, fading as quietly as they came, and winter stills the land again.

The brazen warmth jostles the senses while it stays, upending occupations. In the air is an immediate change: the hum of rural industry. Tree sparrows prepare nests with gathered chaff; onions are buried up to their shoulders in hastily dug plots; woodlarks spiral high to sing their elusive songs, as if liquid were tumbling from nowhere; and rugs are hung to air like an embroidered gallery. Villagers use sickles to sharpen the fat ends of canes, ready to be sunk into summer gardens for climbing beans. A wall lizard clambers over the old beehive; it is smaller than my smallest finger, yet as eager for warmth as I.

The true expressions of spring, though, are few. The trees and meadows are pale with winter, as washed out as a found photograph. The hillsides are sparse, and ice still guards the river edge. The halcyon days are a conjurer's season—a sleight of hand or trick of the light—but no less exuberant for their false promise. In their convivial company you would be forgiven for thinking the end of winter was near, that it was safe to sow tender plants and clean out the wood stove, but that would be mistaking their significance. Rather, it is a time of gifts and small miracles—a brief brumal dance between storms.

The morning was already warm when we set off to climb a mountain that rises above the smaller of the lakes. We followed logging tracks, some still decked with snow, which corkscrewed through dense forest. It was like swerving along a border, in and out of time. The dark valley clefts and shaded woods were still winter-cold, where only a thin frosted light slipped through the lacework of branches, but when we stepped into a clearing, or along a sunward ridge, we were welcomed into spring like a shared celebration. A drowsy southern wind raked the leaves around us, and stubble fires smoldered on the plain below—the coils of smoke lifting like a kettle of cranes.

A few butterflies swooned in the sun: a red admiral wheeled above a reef of leaves; a peacock shyly showed its colors, as if uncertain of its claim; a tortoiseshell festooned a stone. It was their first warmth in months and they swam in it, draping their myriad designs over the pale places of winter. Around the bend, fresh bear tracks crept past us in the crusted snow.

We found the fire salamander in a water tank whose cover had come away. It must have slipped on the stone lip, and drowned beneath the fall of water when it couldn't climb out. Its orange spots floated like fireflies in the dark depths.

The tank collected springwater to supply a village below, and Julia suggested removing the salamander. We looked for something to lift it with, unsure if its skin secretions were harmful. The beech and oak leaves that surrounded us were too small, but a single maple leaf lay conspicuously near, as though its autumn arc had been intended.

It took three tries to scoop the dead salamander from the swirling water. I cradled it on the makeshift raft; its black skin glistened like oil, teardropped with bright flames. A foreleg trembled involuntarily, as if shaking the last of the water off. Then a back leg stuttered forward, followed by the foreleg again. We set it down with a sudden rush of joy. The moment of wonder had been unexpected, a keepsake in the season of gifts. For a few minutes the salamander delicately remembered its limbs, before ambling off with a twirl of its tail into a drift of damp leaves.

On our way down the mountain we heard woodpeckers drumming in the woods. Yellow crocuses had crested the soil to flower in the fugitive light. We walked the last of the valley in wintry shade, knowing the crocuses would soon quiver with cold, or be lost beneath snow. But for now they blazed like a hillside of rare suns.

Among Reeds

THE OLD ADAGE about finding a needle in a haystack could just as easily refer to a bittern in a reed bed. As long as the bittern in question is European, that is. The American bittern, *Botaurus lentiginosus*—as I was amazed to discover on a spring trip to Canada when three of them sailed over a boardwalk in a single morning—is far less secretive than its transatlantic cousin. The European bittern, *Botaurus stellaris*, on the other hand, could be a synonym for *shy*; it is a bird more imagined than seen, and, as such, is spoken of in the same mysterious hush as a hermit.

The bittern is such an elusive bird in part because of the nature of its home. It requires large tracts of dense and undisturbed reed bed, a place to disappear. The bittern's plumage is as enigmatic as its habitat: a cross-hatching of shadow and light, as though zippers of tawny feathers had been sewn into black cloth in an approximation of reeds and dark water. Although it runs the risk of a reed bed drying out, being subsumed in a sudden flood, or icing over in winter, the bittern is monogamous when it comes to place. It's so reluctant to leave, even to be seen, that conservationists estimate their numbers by sound. Each spring the male bittern gives himself away with an eerie foghorn boom that travels clear across immense reed beds in the hope of finding a mate. The call rolls out of the depths, a trembling exhalation of air. When the brief season of song reaches its end, the bittern retires again to its obscurity, a recluse of the reeds.

The common reed, *Phragmites australis*, is a grass—an exceedingly tall, feather-topped blade of grass. This transitional plant belongs to a phase of landscape that occupies the gap between open water and emergent boggy woodland, or carr. It springs up bright green in estuaries and shallow pools, on floodplains and lake edges, quickly colonizing wetland fringes and spreading rapidly through horizontal runners that root themselves along the way. By midsummer the reeds are verdant, a green sea crested with waves of purple flowers that swell in the slightest of breezes. But by the end of the year they are transformed by a golden molt into a field of harvest sheaves.

Only a handful of bird species make reeds their primary home. To come across them is far from certain; to go looking for one is like trying to pry a secret from stone. Once, when walking a sandy strait that meandered through reeds, I heard the song of a Cetti's warbler. For such a small brown bird the call is a startling shimmer that rings clearly through the air. I looked around, hoping to glimpse it darting about the reed litter. I heard a few soft twitterings, a rustling here and there, and finally silence. Stepping into the reeds in the direction of the song, I swept the canes to my sides as if I were swimming through kelp. My shirt snagged on a stem, another threaded itself through the loop of my binocular straps, one hooked me in the ear. I moved forward through a process of persistent twisting. Stumbling over the tough stalks of snapped reeds, their sharp ends stabbed into my shins, shifting me off balance. Rank water leaked over my boots and reed stems crackled loudly underfoot, each step a graceless intrusion.

When I reached the place where I thought the call had come from, the reed bed was silent. A sudden wind passed through, tilting the reeds in an exaggerated bow, as if thanking me for coming. I sensed that something was out there, but knew I would never find it. I retreated awkwardly to the sandy trail strewn with reefs of bone-white shells. Behind me I heard a rustling from among the reeds, then the Cetti's warbler spoke up, loudly scolding me from the exact place I had been. When I turned to look back, the reeds were quietly bowing again.

The way into a reed bed is through silence. Sight quickly loses its status in the dense thicket of stems, sometimes leading one to an exasperated state of mind. Hearing, however, is honed. Even the slenderest of sounds are audible; the faint fluttering of wings is amplified by the quiet, rising up as clearly as voices in an ancient amphitheater.

Some birds can be followed by their song. The bearded reedling, *Panurus biarmicus*, weaves its way in small flocks through the intricate maze to the chorus of a single, brightly polished note, as if the tines of a garden fork were glancing off a series of stones. They usually stay low and unseen in the reeds, heard as only a passing song, but when they trundle up a stem, bending it with their weight as they near the top, they reveal themselves to be the most exquisite of birds.

They appear dressed for an unusual evening out; both the male and female wearing long cinnamon tails. But while she's thrown a white scarf over her wings and a tight rufous cap on her head, he sports a slate-blue hood and old-fashioned mustaches that trail like opposing black commas to his chest. The ensembled birds clamber up the stems together, often straddling two at a time with their thin black legs. They rock back and forth in the wind like dinghies in a breezy bay. Within moments of appearing, though, they are usually gone, hitting the same high lilting note on cue and bounding back into flight through the maze of reeds.

Reed beds are full of cryptic signs: a mussel shell split open near a stone; a faint tunnel furrowed through rush; a found feather or whistlings that shift with the wind. Some signs can be guessed at, like animal hieroglyphics, while others require greater imagination. It's easy enough, however, to imagine things that aren't there.

I'd set out to spend a day in the reed beds. It was mid-November and a clear, warm light spread over the lake basin—one of those rare autumn days when summer seeps back in. The hill slopes were alive with motion: a sparrowhawk sliced past and emptied an oak tree of mistle thrush and jays; a few ragged butterflies bounced between dusty flowers; partridges cannoned from beneath shrubs; and a pair of ravens smudged the sky above. As I neared the lake, I descended an overgrown track through silver birch and willow, then walked out into the brilliance of reeds. They were the color of honey in a window of sun.

The Prespa Lakes, dating back more than five million years, are among the oldest in the world, belonging to a small and select group of ancient water bodies. Their recent loss of water, like the age of a tree, can be gauged by rings of growth, vegetation that has sprung up in the water's wake. As a reed bed dries out, its young runners trail after the retreating lake. The old reeds that remain, brittle from storms and sun, gradually break down to form a layer of organic matter, the perfect base for damp-loving trees like the silver birch and willow I had wandered past. And so rings are formed: reeds following water, trees following reeds.

I walked on a sandy trail that was once lake bed before it was beach. Now it was a path through reeds. The scattered shells of its earlier incarnation shone like an archipelago of salt isles. Above them floated ferny grasses on nearly invisible stems. Insects hummed in the air, and the sun bore down on me. The reed bed was vast, broken only in places by a few stunted trees, spaced like a kind of loneliness.

I'd been wandering for about an hour through the brimming heat when I stopped to drink water from my flask. I lay back on the sand in the warmth of the stolen season and stared up at a ribbon of blue sky. Out of the silence came a sudden, terrifying wail. I bolted up and listened carefully. It came again, piercing and piglike, a haunting siren-squeal. The cry lifted hairs on the back of my neck; I had once seen a wild boar protectively herd nearly a dozen of her young from the edge of the lake, so I knew the animal could easily be near. I packed my flask quickly away and edged toward the mass of pale stems. The sunlight was bright in my eyes, and the next shuddering wail echoed within me.

I pushed into the reeds, simultaneously thrilled and terrified by what I might find. To surprise a wild boar in these murky depths would be unwise, I knew, but it was an opportunity I couldn't let go. So rare is it to encounter the larger European mammals that such a moment is charged with an instinctive pull. I pressed on as quietly as I could, every few steps being startled again by the curdling cries. When I reached deeper into the reed bed it was still pooled with stale water, clotted with bulrushes and tussocks of sedge. The reeds swayed in the humid breeze, rattling like raked leaves.

The next screech was near, close by in the dark, watery tangle. I stood motionless and heard something approaching. Directly in front of me came a rustling and snapping of stems, a few dim plops in the turbid water. Reed stalks shivered with each of its steps. I could see nothing but the bending of stems, and began wondering why I'd planted myself like a statue in the animal's way.

A bearded reedling momentarily distracted me as it landed near my head, a sudden and fleeting beauty. I felt my heart hammering, and quickly returned my attention to the oncoming creature. When a second and third bearded reedling perched close by and edged up a stem, though, I paused and refocused my thoughts.

A vague remark returned to me, something I'd read or been told, but had forgotten over time. It concerned the water rail, *Rallus aquaticus*, a bird that humbly patrols the marine world of reeds. I remembered something about its remarkable voice and smiled to myself, recalling the description of "a squealing pig" and "explosively loud." I felt a great relief, and unexpected joy, as a few more bearded reedlings showed up and seemed oblivious to my presence. When the first group departed, a second arrived. I noticed that each flock was taking off from the bundled rushes I'd been watching for the boar, and suddenly realized that the illusion had been conjured by two different birds. While the water rail had squealed from the rushes, the bearded reedlings were busily bending and crackling the stems as they clambered along them, preparing for takeoff. Now they were arriving in squadrons, wave after wave of them, nimbly swinging on stems like a troupe of painted acrobats whirling around my head. They shuffled toward the tasseled ends, balancing with their tails, and unstitched the pillows of seed as they fed. More and more arrived—as many as 150 I would later guess—and with each flutter of wings and needlework of beak the air around me was filled with delicate pale down. When the last of the birds had departed, the wisps of floating seed were all that convinced me that it hadn't been a dream. For a few minutes I listened for the water rail, but the world was submerged.

✿

What often strikes me about reed beds are the possibilities for transformation. Each time I enter one, I sense a change take place. I move more slowly and openly, with a focused clarity, aware of the slightest of signs. It is as if no other place had ever existed; every subtle sensation belongs to that singular, wild terrain. When sunlight in high summer pours over the crackling stems, or a wind murmurs through the leaves, a breathlessness about reeds stills time, allowing room for reflection.

A number of the birds that inhabit reed beds are blessed with the ability to transform themselves, as if the habitat itself had alchemical designs. The water rail, so shy and unassuming, rarely seen as it spends its days skulking through dense cover, is a ventriloquist of great skill. Its repertoire of calls, as I now know, covers a range of identities, scarcely believable when the bird is actually observed. The water rail seems unexceptional, even comical at first sight. It is as small as a fowl and waddles on squat orange legs. Against a sleek, blue-gray breast and face, its long red bill seems borrowed from someone else. And when it scurries into reeds, a fluffed white rump is often all that is seen. Its polyphonic calls are all the more startling for their incongruity, their brash unexpectedness.

The bearded reedling can change the way it eats. Throughout summer it feasts on the bounty of insects that thrum around reeds. In winter, though, instead of migrating to warmer regions where it could still find its food of choice, it alters the workings of its stomach. It adapts itself to accommodate the plentiful reed seeds and vegetable matter of its year-round home. Its gizzard thickens and puts on weight, and the bird consumes large amounts of sand and grit to help grind up tough vegetable fiber. With the emergence of insects in spring, the bird's metamorphosis comes full circle.

The bittern, as the most secretive of reed bed species, is unsurprisingly an expert at camouflage. Along with suitable plumage, its particular transformative skill is to replicate a reed. When necessary it will lift its black and tawny neck high into the air so that its long tapered bill points skyward, a reed stem among many. It can maintain this posture for up to an hour, motionlessly blending into the background, its black and yellow eye fastened on threats.

On two occasions I've been fortunate enough to observe the European bittern. Each time it was in the depths of a harsh winter, and the birds had been flushed from their homes by ice. When a reed bed freezes over, the bittern loses access to the fish, frogs, and eels that make up most of its diet and is forced to look elsewhere; each of the birds I have watched stalked the iceless perimeter of a lake. They stepped through the open water on flamboyant green legs, slicing their sharp bills through the surface to feed. Every so often they abruptly stopped, as if sensing an encroaching threat. The bitterns tilted their heads like an opening drawbridge and then spiked their bills toward the sky, as if they were puppets controlled by strings from above. For a few moments they stayed as still as the reeds that no longer encircled them; even their wary eyes seemed iced into place. Eventually they relaxed and began wading through the shallows again. Despite the empty surface of water, the reed bed was carried in their minds.

Reed beds have long been places to disappear into, so conducive are they to secrecy. Smugglers along the coasts of Britain in the eighteenth and nineteenth centuries often stowed their barrels of bootleg brandy and rum in them rather than risk houses as hideaways. Once you step inside, something closes behind you, as if a shawl had been drawn over the world, islanding you alone. The feathered denizens of this realm are the recluses of the avian orders. They shun the outside world, entering it only when necessary, and as briefly as possible.

The places birds go can be difficult to navigate, but reed beds are more than just somewhere to roam. They are reflective, meditative spaces, where the din of crowded lives can be lost for a while. It has occurred to me that the bittern's strange transformation into a reed in open water serves no practical purpose. It seems contradictory and vaguely ridiculous—puzzling at the very least. But it is simply displaying its true nature, regardless of location. There are times, amidst the shrill clamor of streets and cities, the grasping congestion of time, when I have reached for the remembered stillness discovered among reeds, tried to preserve it beyond that landscape's range. Perhaps the bittern in open water has recalled its own equilibrium.

To be surrounded by tall reeds narrows the sky above. It concentrates the clouds and clarifies the mind. I have often come looking for reedlings and rails but found something else instead—the still center of self. It is there in the mystery of what invisibly moves, the hushed and tilting winds, the oceanic light. I rarely glimpse the most solitary of birds—it is enough to pass through, knowing they are there.

Time in the Karst Country

THIS HIGH, ROLLING PLATEAU is wedded to water, though that's not easy to divine. Other than a month or two of flaring spring flowers drawn from winter's lingering well, the karst country assumes an aspect of drought. No streams silver the valleys, no pools or ponds collect snapshots of the sky—just a sun-raked expanse of dry and lilting hills shimmering into the distance, a place of stone and swept grasses, wild tantrums of dust.

I dip a hand into a stone bowl and fish out a few grains of lichen, ash-gray and flecked with jade; they're blown easily from my fingers by a breeze. A deep rent in the stone surface beside me shelters a stunted wild rose, its single scarlet hip the fruit of its meager season. Sliding my finger into a limestone fissure, I feel the chalky abrasions that are the relics of an ancient sea.

Limestone is largely composed of the fragmented remains of marine organisms, the compressed microskeletons and shells of antique sea creatures dating from when this land lay beneath an ocean. As though in fidelity to its origins, limestone is also soluble: it lets water in, so that the stones scattered about me are all gradually dissolving, each fluted channel and etched meander, each steep abyss and overhanging lip the result of rock being rinsed away.

Looking up, I see limestone spilling over the hills, rising up the ridges in serried walls or fallen to the hollows. The sculpted silver rocks are the essence of karst, a landscape characterized by worn and porous limestone or dolomite that's being continually reshaped into new and arising designs. It's a place of disordered complexity, where each singular surface spread out across the plateau contains a range of permutations like the ones beside me. The infinitely slow artistry of water.

✿

I'm alone, and waiting for birds. When they come—singing in the near dark or fledging from the meadows—I record their names and details, then transcribe their positions, heights, and flight paths onto a series of maps. By the end of the day, the maps are cross-hatched and circled with lines, some arrowing to the very edge of the page, others curving with the thermals into a gradually expanding helix. The result of the many pencil marks is a complex cartography of space, revealing the ways in which the birds that breed and hunt on the plateau use the very air itself, and what might happen if something were to alter that emptiness.

That something is a series of fiberglass blades spinning with the wind. An energy company envisages twenty-four turbines standing in three orderly rows atop the ridges, reaching 120 meters high with a blade span 80 meters wide. Alternative energy bears associated costs, just as with conventional forms of production. Collisions and casualties caused by wind turbines are not uncommon, particularly amongst species that rely on thermals for their slow, circling flights such as pelicans, storks, eagles, and other large raptors. Breeding territories are also susceptible to disruption when the accompanying infrastructure is trucked in on roads newly carved out of sensitive habitat, resulting in decline, dispersion, and occasionally even the disappearance of a rare bird or plant.

Julia is invisible beyond a steepled ridge, rooted to a vantage point on the highest shelf of the plateau. Hired to survey the birds of the area, we're spending forty-five days in these limestone hills spread out over the seasons, compiling the data for an environmental assessment that will determine the likely ecological impact of the proposed wind park. Working from a series of observation points and line transects walked at different times of the day, we chart the movements and kinds of birds we encounter, but as in any situation that affords the opportunity for intimacy with place, the birds are only part of a larger, illuminating entity. Whole days can pass in the karst country without seeing a soul, the ridges ebbing away in the haze. Here, secluded at the very edge of Greece, less than an hour's walk from Albania, our phones rarely work; their signals, like our view of each other, are blotted out by the undulating land. So we are left alone with the stone and arched sky, the mysterious winds and clamor of wings, the unending passage of time.

☼

Scanning the sky I find a short-toed eagle floating at the end of the telescope. I look up into the vast blue vault with just my eyes to try and fix the bird's position against the land, but it's far too high to place clearly. Returning to the telescope, I catch the eagle before it falls, parachuting down without any discernible effort. Its legs hang like loose tassels, the dark muzzle of its head tipped forward. The pale wings are swept back and angled in such a way that they carve through the air unhindered. The bird would be sinking if this were still a sea.

I follow the eagle as it plummets, growing larger with each moment. The blue sky blurs into a backdrop of grassy hills, and then stones begin to focus in the telescope as the distance to the ground rapidly narrows. When the eagle pulls up, its wings flaring into a pair of speckled fans, it is only a second shy of the earth. Feeding almost exclusively on snakes, the coiled or shifting target spied from an immense height must have slithered away a moment before the spiked impact of talons. The eagle brakes on the air and waits, floating with the span of its deeply fingered wings while it eyes the empty grass. I keep watch alongside it, but know there are things I'll never see.

Two hundred and forty-five million years ago the land spread out around the eagle and I lay on the floor of the Tethys Ocean, a vast body of water suspended between the ancient supercontinents of Gondwana and Laurasia. The debris of dead marine organisms settled in deep reefs on the seabed were compacted and transformed over the course of another seventy million years into solid, sedimentary stone. When the ancient land masses eventually began shifting toward one another, the limestone deposits layered beneath the Tethys Ocean to a depth of four hundred meters experienced a period of intense pressure; they were played like a concertina between the continents. The ocean floor buckled and staggered inexorably upwards, driven by the force of displacing tectonic plates until the water drained steadily away, eventually bringing mountains into the sky and transporting this limestone seabed to the surface.

The short-toed eagle drives its wings through the air, working them like bellows. It's so near that I can make out the black centers to its fire-swept eyes when it raises its head from the empty ground. The eagle turns my way and heaves forward, wavering over the mounds and hollows to the rise and fall of its wings. Its sheer size becomes apparent in proximity to the wildflowers and scattered shrubs shrinking beneath it. I watch it glide over the grasses, and I'm struck by being caught up in a process, part of a vast continuum spanning stone and sea. However brief the life of an eagle, however frail my own, we coexist in this moment within a stream of time unwinding, in a place both eroding and reshaped, transformed as it wears away. The poet W. H. Auden had a deep fascination for karst landscapes, believing that we are attracted to them because of our shared mutability. He proclaimed us "the inconstant ones," and so is all of this.

The wondrous quality of karst is dependent on dissolution. The limestone dissolves around its joints, the cracks and fissures present in the stone at its creation millions of years ago. Progressively enlarged they form grykes, the deep vertical grooves where the wild rose was harbored, along with the blocks and pavements of intricately etched stone in between called clints. The land is so porous that water vanishes swiftly through the myriad crevices, leaving the plateau nearly as dry as before, each rainfall further encoding its aridity.

Along with being weathered from above, limestone is dissolved by circulating groundwater, hollowed out so that caverns and aquifers develop below. In places the ground slumps without the support of bedrock until sinkholes, or dolines, pockmark the land as though it had been hit by a storm of fallen meteors. The karst country is labyrinthine as a result; it dips and furrows into the distance, like the very sea turned to stone.

The short-toed eagle veers away from me, tilting its wings to disappear into a doline. Emerging over the opposite rim it steers off across the plateau. I watch it cleave to the buckled country, sailing over the rocky crests.

Each sound in the karst country is amplified into a near presence. They are more than merely audible, within the frail and narrow range of human hearing, but give shape to invisible things. When a summer wind rakes the grasses it ignites with a whisper, a vague and uncertain ceremony performed in the distance. The sound gathers strength before sweeping over the hillsides, a rising murmur that precedes the arched and waving grasses. When the wind song fades away a few stalks still quiver in its wake.

Deepened by the surrounding silence, the sounds of the plateau appear initially without source, sovereign articulations of the air. The persistent song of a quail springs from the deep grasses to echo and reverberate between the hills and the sky like a prayer bell rung from a mountaintop. I hear alpine swifts long before I see them, a circling susurration that seems to arrive from all directions, and I unexpectedly tense when they scythe above me in a ribbon of trembling wings. Invisible raptors beg from the cliffs, their plaintive cries rising while alpine choughs squabble playfully on high, uttering a strange incantation of mechanical squawks. The songs always reach me before their forms darken the sky.

The bells of a herd floated close one afternoon. I couldn't see the animals, hidden as they were in one of the myriad valleys that unroll between the hills, but the dull clanging of their bells came and went with the wind. Mountain clouds swirled in and shifted darkly overhead, a leaden pall spreading like smoke across the plateau. When another sound joined the bells, I realized a shepherd was accompanying the herd with a flute. Invisible to me, his song swirled around like the rain-heavy clouds, floating near and then far. I listened to the shepherd's song for some minutes, its tender and ethereal beauty reflecting the wandering of paths, until it slipped into a further valley, blown away like grass seeds about the hills again.

To walk the highest ridge is to enter the realm of kestrels, a wind-rilled place of stone-encircled mounts and sinkholes where these elegant raptors breed in the clefts and crannies of cliffs. By the end of summer, when the fledglings have joined their elders in the air, the kestrels hunt over the hillsides in large but scattered numbers so that they keep appearing on the horizon like the rising and falling horses of a merry-go-round. They glide out of the blinding sun, a cinnamon shimmer swiftly glancing above or arrowing up the valley, sheering across the grasslands to turn sharply in the air and suddenly still themselves. The kestrel's particular hunting technique—its graceful and hypnotic hover—requires the rapt attention associated with emptying the mind. Amidst the wild beating of its wings, the bird's eyes remain perfectly still and in position, focused on the ground and possible prey. Film studies have shown that a kestrel's eyes move less than six millimeters in any direction while it hovers, each shift occasioned by the wind compensated for by another—the dipping of the tail, the forward stretch of its neck, a momentary delay of wings.

The suspended cruciforms of kestrels stand out against the sky; the hovering birds mark my route, like an avenue of trees or deliberate cairns. They also delineate the line of intended turbines, both bird and blade seeking the wind that wells and funnels about the mountain crests for their endeavors. So I walk the stony ridge recording all that I see or hear on both sides: the flame-colored tails of black redstarts extinguishing upon landing; wheatears nodding from the rocks; the songs of ortolan buntings, an avian variation of Beethoven's Fifth, pulsing through the murmuring air. Rock nuthatches dip like shy children behind boulders, and the slate-blue heads and rust-red bellies of rock thrushes flash from afar. Many of the ridgeline birds are uncommon or nonexistent in other habitats, but they are supremely suited to karst, at home in a world of stone.

My transect line is meant to be straight, but I'm continually being forced to amend it, swinging wide around sudden pillars and prominences, skirting boulders and ankle-twisting scree. I let the stones guide me instead, detailing my route to their designs. Whichever way they lead me in spring, each step brings butterflies spilling from the grasses. Until the land dries up in midsummer they tremble about my knees in myriad numbers, their brief season of flight coinciding with the frail tenure of flowers. Marbled whites, peacocks, and great banded graylings. Orange-tips, blues, and clouded yellows. All the names of the color range drifting ahead of me.

Skylark song rains down with the sunlight when I find the bomb casing. It's the color of autumn beech leaves and wedged amongst stones. I kneel down and edge my head toward the opening at one end of the shell and peer inside a dark and hollow chamber. But when I lay a tentative finger to the nose cone it feels dense to my touch. I have no idea what time and weather do to the ingredients of ordnance, what elements might have leached away or become undone by water, what might remain packed inside the tapered tip, but enough reminders of the Greek Civil War lay scattered about the land that a corroded casing leaves me feeling uneasy.

From the ridge I can see clear across the plateau. Winding tracks disappear into the sea of stone or vanish around bends in the hills. It is a mysterious, mazelike landscape, furnished with secrets despite its evident emptiness. Trying to pry open the intimacies of its human history is a complicated task. The fierce battles that flared across these northern parts of Greece seem remote, alien and unreachable, a thing of the past. Yet the last dying days of the routed Communist soldiers, fleeing refugees and abandoned villages, were only sixty years ago. A speck in the span of time. Gun emplacements still guard the hillsides, flower-filled hemispheres of mounded rocks. Stone-walled storerooms crouch low in the sinkholes, where shrubs have taken hold away from wind and underground tunnels web the ridgeline, anchored at their ends by slumped bunkers.

While it's common in the narratives of war for the nonhuman world to be overshadowed, I find myself thinking about birds when I pass the memorial mounds of stone. The species I encounter most days—rock thrushes and woodlarks, wheatears and black redstarts, skylarks and linnets—would have made use of the same places they still do, and witnessed a violently divided people at close range. While men piled stones against strafing, or oiled guns in the secrecy of a sinkhole, the birds would have continued to lay claim in their usual way, building nests and raising young, hunting across the karst country with an abiding and insistent purpose. And when bombs dropped from the sky, the birds would have shredded as easily as men.

☼

In his book *The Wild Places*, Robert Macfarlane traces W. H. Auden's fascination with limestone back to his native Pennine shires of northern England, where karst landscapes are common: "What most moved him about it was the way it eroded." Worn away at its weakest points, Macfarlane notes that it is these "first flaws" in limestone that determine its future shape, becoming deep-rooted characteristics as they enlarge over time. "For Auden, this was a human as well as a geological quality: he found in limestone an honesty—an acknowledgement that we are as defined by our faults as by our substance."

Those faults can take many forms, some cast down to us by circumstance, others inherited with the particular worlds we are born into. I met Stavros as he strode down a hillside with a staff in one hand and a black dog padding faithfully beside him. It was early morning but an intense heat already hazed the air. He was born only a few kilometers away, but on the "wrong side of the border" according to the shepherd, meaning Albania. After nearly half a century of brutal dictatorship, characterized by sealed borders, secret police, and entrenched poverty, Stavros left his home after the fall of the Communist state in the early 1990s. Already in his midforties by then, he told his father he was "going on the road to look for work." Stavros has since spent nineteen years in Greece, the last fourteen of them working for a Greek cattle farmer on the plateau. From dawn until dusk, from early spring until the first snows of winter, the shepherd ranges the limestone hills with his herd, seeking out the scarce green grasses that remain alive in the sinkholes. In the evenings he cooks for himself on a fire of split oak outside the tent where he sleeps. But until he can retire in a few years, Stavros passes his days and nights alone while his wife and family live in a Greek city forty kilometers to the south. Now that he is in his sixties, the rarity of a regular job in a land of migrant labor is too good to give up and so he endures the isolation of the karst country.

While standing in the shade of a tree I asked Stavros if he played the flute. He smiled in reply. Sliding the homemade instrument from his satchel, he told me that he played the accordion and clarinet as well but kept them at his home in the city. The clear notes that lifted with his fingers woke the still and quiet dawn, hushed and dreamlike in the brimming day, and I recalled the song that had swirled around me on that earlier occasion, the fragile beauty of its shape, its invisible performer. I could now see the deep creases that marked the shepherd's face as the song resolved into air, the sunken laugh lines that rivered his forehead and the skin on his hands that had the look of cracked glass. There is a singular distinctiveness brought about by weathering and ageing, both limestone and ourselves the inconstant ones, enduring the elements, overcoming the flaws of our inheritance. Dissolution is more than a lessening; it's a reminder of time worn well.

It's not easy imagining our place in the geologic span. The measurements are unforgiving, vast sets of numerals like the numbing multitude of galaxies and stars in existence; few of our minds are attuned to such sublime and inconsolable figures. In 1830 the Scotsman Charles Lyell published the first volume of his influential book, *The Principles of Geology*, proposing that the Earth's features were the result of immeasurably slow and gradual forces still in operation today. A window onto the planet's past suddenly opened, and the view was staggering. Building upon the ideas of James Hutton, his theory upended the general consensus of the age: that the history of the Earth could be measured in terms of human generations, and that its physical properties were the result of violent planetary cataclysms occurring during that short span. Instead Lyell suggested that infinitesimal changes, accumulating over vast periods of time, were responsible for the geological appearance of the planet, conceding that Earth might in fact be far older than previously thought, perhaps many millions, even hundreds of millions of years old.

Geological discoveries recalibrated the scale of existence as we perceive it, much as Charles Darwin's theory of evolution did again some thirty years after Lyell's book. Although we now know more about the Earth's origins and probable demise than early geologists could ever have ascertained, including its age of around four and a half billion years, the assertion of James Hutton in 1788 that the planet appeared to have "no vestige of a beginning—no prospect of an end" remains existentially accurate.

The karst country conveys this timelessness through its terrain: the indifferent duration of stone. Although there are scattered trees in the gullies and an oak grove rooted to the center of the plateau, it is the wilder, treeless, more austere regions that carry the unique and mysterious signature of limestone. Though outliving humans by hundreds and sometimes thousands of years, trees remain comfortably familiar to us through their comparable mortal spans. A tree's lifetime—in comparison to that of stone—is roughly commensurate with one's own: we share a kindred insignificance. It is the karst country that unfolds into immensity.

As I walk the last of the ridge, I feel an affinity with stone. Along with my concerns for the future of birds on the plateau—their flight patterns more fragile than I'd imagined—the place has absorbed me into its pattern. I'm encircled by an expanse of dissolving land, an entrancing work of water worn away over ineffable ages beneath the same passing sun. And over the months I've understood this landscape's capacity to alter my perception. It has opened me to the unfathomable beauty of distance and deep time, but also proximity: the things revealed when we draw near. How the envious solidity of stone is also inconstant, its eroding designs as rich as a shepherd's weathered smile.

The stones sing as the sun begins to fall. There is a quality to the karst country light that is mesmeric, spilling over the grasslands, bathing the ridges and rolling hills in a deep and reflective radiance. It is as though it were a relic luminescence, a memory of when this plateau was still an ocean; that in the compacted shells of the marine creatures that have surfaced into stone there remains a trace of what was pelagic about them, an alloyed and ethereal echo of sunlight striking sea.

A kestrel leans from the sky to hover ahead of me. There's a bloom of light on its wings, an intense shard of color balanced like water on the edge of a leaf. The bird reflects the passage of stone: it is still and in motion at the same moment, poised with equal weight between two seemingly opposing states. It harnesses the air with patient and deliberate precision. Moving and unmoved. I watch it still its quivering wings before it drops, like a stone through the sea, as I slope off the hills into evening.

The Distance between Us

I have kept asking myself . . . what the invisible connections
that determine our lives are, and how the threads run.

    W. G. SEBALD, *Campo Santo*

NOW AND THEN I see him again, though I never know precisely
when the moment might be. He has a tendency to arrive unan-
nounced. For nearly seventeen years our relationship has existed
this way, fugitive and unreliable. But it remains charged with such
significance that I'm willing to forgive its frustrations. We rendez-
vous on his terms, not mine, and always in the same remembered
place. It's a whale-backed hill overlooking Morecambe Bay, and
the season is never anything but spring.

I'd been living amidst the moors of northern England when
I first saw him. Having some time off work, and feeling restless
in the unfurling days of May, I traveled by train to the coast.
Morecambe Bay is a vast and changeable terrain on the edge of
Cumbria where water and sand verge on the indivisible, trading natures throughout the night and day. At low tide the sand
ripples into the distance until the far ribbon of sea glistens and
shines like the lights of an island. There is nothing solid about this
coastal composition; the bay is constantly shifting, unsettled in its
essence. When the sea begins its return it infiltrates the sand, slipping between acres of grains and sparking alchemical processes
as it goes.

My train slowed above a sweep of red-streaked mud, crossing the causeway that spans the northern end of the bay. I found a room for the night in an odd, neo-gothic hotel in the quiet retirement town of Grange-over-Sands. Despite being lodged at the far end of the top, turreted floor, I seemed to be the only guest haunting the long hallways.

After dinner I asked the owner if he could recommend a walk for the following day. He seemed pleased with the possibility for conversation, and showed me obligingly to an armchair in the lounge. Some minutes later he returned carrying a bottle of single malt cradled in his hand, two clinking glasses, and a map. Over the course of the evening, and the diminishing whiskey, he proposed a number of routes, but one struck me as particularly appealing. It began at the edge of town, where a ridge of rounded hills could be walked in one of two directions. If I made my way east, the owner told me, I could cut down one of the side valleys to a village pub serving home-brewed ales. In the glow of the late-evening whiskey, his suggestion settled the matter with ease.

I left the hotel early, spring light beginning to skim the bay. Gulls arrowed over the seafront and the first of the day's therapeutic strolls started up along the promenade. I soon found the edge of town and felt the keen tingle that comes with walking in springtime. A dry stone wall crept up an emerald meadow and I followed its stride. It might have been there for centuries, yet its stones had stayed true to their precise and allotted sockets, as if the wall had pushed through the earth intact. Wildflowers unfolded with the morning, tiny dabs of promise scattered over the swelling green sward. A salt breeze stole up behind me, and I glimpsed it disappearing into the meadow grass, riffling through like a village rumor.

Somewhere on the way up, I turned to look back. The pewter and blue wash of Morecambe Bay shimmered away from me. It was midtide, so that much of the sands were still exposed, or glazed with a translucent, sunburst sheen. From high above I could make out the various patterns inscribed by an earlier incursion. Strange codes encrypted the shore: tide pools like blue eyes, long serrated reefs, cirques opening here and there. The waterscape entranced, the whole bay mimicking a minor archipelago.

But its appearance was deceptive—over time the bay has claimed many lives, those unable to compass their way back over the shifting, water-filling sands.

I spun away from the bright bay and followed the stone wall that led me up the slope. Reaching the top, I could see a range of hills strung out ahead of me. Each one rose and fell gently, as though surfacing for air. Wind and wild grasses had bequeathed them a sinuous shape, unbroken by boulders or trees. Where each hill fell away a smooth saddle held them together. Warmth filled the morning and a clear, burnished glow drifted from the sky, layering the grassy swells in light.

Some way ahead of me I saw a man walking east. He leaned a little to one side, as though being aided by a cane. Despite the distance that lay between us, his presence was conspicuous atop the buckled ridge: nothing else broke the horizon of the hills, and his clothes were the color of pitch.

The morning slowed while I walked, buoyed by the light, and the tender spring grasses gave way easily underfoot. Judging from his hesitant steps, and the distinctive black suit he wore walking, I imagined the man in the distance to be elderly, carrying the elegant airs of a more decorous time. Although following in his wake, I had the sense that we were walking the hills together, hoving in and out of view with the dipping and rising of the ridges. When I surfaced from one of the saddles he would be sloping down the next. Our paths were entwined in this way, this ebb and flow, this rise and fall, constant as the sea's slow advancing seep.

The distance between us gradually lessened. I'd closed the gap until I was near enough to make out the man's limp more clearly. He had to hitch his left leg, as if to swing it over a tangle of barbed wire, before he could steer it behind the other. Over the years his hair had thinned a little on top, so that it hung in a dark disc above his ears. But the most striking aspect of his appearance was his black suit, matched by a pair of polished shoes: it seemed to react to the sun, radiating a dark luminescence as if lit from within. The man walked the furrowed hills alone, distinguished by sunlight. And I followed his every shining step.

I watched him slope into the next hollow, disappearing from view in the usual way, like a seabird sliding from a crest. But this time he didn't surface; the sun-washed grasses rippled without him where I'd expected his ascent. He must have finally tired, I reckoned, imagining him seated somewhere on the saddle, dabbing his brow with a folded white handkerchief. But there was no sign of him when a few minutes later I reached the saddle myself. Great swathes of open meadow fell away to either side. Dark trees and villages studded the far valleys, but nothing stirred within sight. I scouted both sides of the hollow and then combed the flanking slopes. I ran on to the lip of the next hill and looked back over the route we'd just traversed, seeing how it curled in the distance toward the bright and shining sea. I turned around to scan the empty path that lay ahead of me, knowing it had been altered forever. The man was nowhere to be seen, and no sign of his passage lingered. He'd simply vanished into sunlight.

☼

The man on the hill returns from time to time, as brightly lit in memory as on the hills above Morecambe Bay. In many ways he has changed the course of my life. They may seem minor and insignificant abstractions, like inconsequential grains of sand let fall through one's hand, but together they carry a weight, a solidity that keeps him grounded close by.

Each time I'm out walking and gain a hilltop ridge I unthinkingly scan its length for a dark, perambulating figure, hoping he has come back to me. I've exhausted long hours and days of my life delving without consequence into the mystery of his disappearance. And at odd and unforeseen moments—talking with friends over wine, sowing seeds in the garden, reading by the fire—I find him slipping easily into my company. The image of him walking the sunlit hills ahead of me arises, locking into place like a closing door. But during these unexpected visits I remember that he's always there, not coming and going via the door, but at home within. He's taken up residence in my memories.

What fascinates me about the man on the hill, however, is not who he was or where he went—though I confess to an unresolved curiosity on both fronts—but the nature of our relationship. Strangers can pass into significance after brief, nearly intangible encounters, courtesy of crossed paths and shared situations, a tenuous glance across a rain-scented street, a lit window revealing a midnight smile, an overheard conversation that lingers after leaving. I've sometimes asked myself how often we enter the lives of strangers, where we're recollected from time to time without our knowing, unaware, even, of the circumstances of our exchange. Are each of us accounted for in the life of another, held there in memory like the man on the hill is in mine, conjured from the thin spring air like a lost counterpart or spiritual sibling, a suggestion of life's myriad turns never taken? We brush against one another with the ease of a wind—occasionally traces must catch.

※

Some years ago I traveled from Prespa to Romania by train. After hours of indecision I finally choose W. G. Sebald's book *The Emigrants* as my companion for the long journey. *The Emigrants* is a beautifully haunting work. In it Sebald sketches four dislocated lives and guides us through a minor compendium of their emigrant memories and intimate habits, their passions and losses, their obsessions. Layer upon layer of detail is built into these stories, including black-and-white images—snapshots of people, domestic interiors, postcards and portraits, ticket stubs and newspaper clippings—but at the heart of each life remains a small knot that can't be unraveled.

I began the book as my train pulled out of Thessaloníki near midnight. I read for a couple of hours before switching off the overhead lamp to drift in and out of sleep as the train sped up and then slowed, sped up and slowed, rattling through the dark countryside. By morning we were in Sofia, and I returned to the book. Throughout the day, while crossing the pale, late-winter plains of northern Bulgaria, watching the low light flare off the swirling brown water of the Danube River, and rumbling past the oil derricks of southern Romania, I fell deeper and deeper into the lives of the emigrants. But something else caught my eye, and it reminded me of the man on the hill: an enigmatic stranger passes through each of the stories.

Vladimir Nabokov was both a well-known writer and a noted lepidopterist, along with being an emigrant himself, having left revolutionary Russia with his parents in 1919 for a life that eventually took him to England, Germany, the United States, and Switzerland. Sebald conjures Nabokov not as a famous author but rather as an ordinary, if magnetic, individual whose life briefly coincides with those of the characters in the book. Staying true to the chronology and geography of the writer's life, Nabokov appears as a ghostlike apparition, minor and easily unnoticed, but there all the same, hovering like a translucent presence, woven into these imagined lives.

Nabokov first appears near the beginning of the book in a heavily shadowed, black-and-white photograph, almost a silhouette. He is standing on a ridge in the Swiss mountains, wearing a white hat tilted back on his head and carrying a butterfly net wedged beneath his right arm. What struck me about the photo was its strange resemblance to the place where I'd last seen the man on the hill. While Nabokov peers at something in the hazy distance, I found myself staring at the eerily analogous backdrop, a long sunken valley slipping away from the ridge and studded with dark trees.

In Nabokov's later appearances he is unnamed, and unknown to the characters whose lives he enigmatically enters. A woman recalls visiting a relative some thirty years earlier in a sanatorium in Ithaca, New York. She recollects looking through the patient's window at the same moment that "a middle-aged man appeared, holding a white net on a pole in front of him and occasionally taking curious jumps." Separated from the incident by three decades, she retains this bright memory of a stranger who passed briefly through her life. The patient follows her gaze into the grounds of the sanatorium and says, "It's the butterfly man, you know. He comes round here quite often."

In another of the stories a painter recalls climbing a mountain above Lake Geneva when "a man of about sixty suddenly appeared before him— like someone who's popped out of the bloody ground. He was carrying a large white gauze butterfly net." The painter is so struck by the appearance of this stranger that he applies his artistry to a portrait, entitled *Man with a Butterfly Net*. The artist is ultimately dismayed by his work, as it "conveyed not even the remotest impression of the strangeness of the apparition it referred to."

Later a character recalls passing two distinguished Russian gentlemen, "one of whom . . . was speaking seriously to a boy of about ten who had been chasing butterflies," while walking with friends in a German park in 1910. The man talking to the boy is recognized by one of the group as Sergei Muromtsev, who four years earlier had been elected president of Russia's first parliament, the Duma. The other man is Nabokov's father, while the boy is Nabokov himself. It is a scene lifted directly from the writer's auto-biography, *Speak, Memory*, but what Sebald has done is to imagine the other lives intersecting at the same time, revealing the scene from another angle. Later in life, Sebald's character returns to the image of the young boy, durably stored away and still shining, when she is proposed to by a man considered unsuitable by her father. In that moment, "though every-thing else around me blurred, I saw that long-forgotten Russian boy as clearly as anything, leaping about the meadows with his butterfly net; I saw him as a messenger of joy, returning from that distant summer day to open his specimen box and release the most beautiful red admirals, peacock butterflies, brimstones and tortoiseshells to signal my final liberation." The relic memory of a briefly seen stranger finds its place in her life again. Inexplicably entwined, their paths converge a second time. The signifi-cance of small moments is to be found in their span; our lives are fashioned from such accretions.

I took a break from reading *The Emigrants* while the train crossed the south-ern plains of Romania. Opening the door to my cabin, I stepped into a corridor of bright windows. The sun was draining from the western sky, laying a last wash of ochre light over the flatlands. Scattered oil derricks rose and fell into the distance, and the grasslands spilled away like the sands of Morecambe Bay. I watched the landscape slip by, my thoughts wrapped up in Nabokov's ghostly appearances and the way the man on the hill still walked ahead of me despite the distance of so many years.

Arms clasped me suddenly about the waist while I stood at the open window, cinching me tight. A rollicking laughter fluttered somewhere by my ear, and I felt a trembling fear rise within. But I swung round in panic to meet the face of a friend. For a few seconds the two of us stood rooted, smiling idiotically at each other until I'd regained my calm. Then we embraced deeply.

Vasillis is Siberian, a wandering writer and painter who'd lived for some time in a village in Prespa. From time to time we'd share a drink at a taverna or chat along the lakeshore where he liked to jog. But we hadn't seen each other for a few years, and when our excitement finally settled down I asked him if he'd just boarded the train. "No, I've been on since Thessaloníki," he said.

"In which carriage?"

"This one. That's my cabin there." Vasillis turned to point to the sleeping compartment next to mine. "Why? Where's yours?" he asked. I smiled and pointed to the adjacent berth, and then we laughed and embraced again in the rolling, sunset corridor.

Like me, Vasillis was traveling to Bucharest, but only long enough to change trains for the Black Sea coast. It was already dark when we pulled in, and he had barely minutes to catch his connection. Watching him dash madly down the corridor, and then weave through the convening crowds, I realized how easily we might have missed one another. If either of our destinations had been earlier in the day we would have stepped off without knowing. Had we emerged from our cabins at alternative times, or waited on the steps by the carriage doors to gain a few precious seconds on our fellow passengers, we would never have understood how closely our paths had crossed. Human lives must be filled with such near misses.

I took a last look in our cabins before leaving, and couldn't help noticing how the spaces were arranged differently. Vasillis's cabin was the mirror image of mine next door, so that our beds were in fact pushed together, separated by only a thin, simple wall. While the train had coursed the dark countryside we had slept as near as lovers, oblivious and dreaming, lost to our own secret worlds.

I stepped down from the train. The brakes hissed and water dripped to the oily tracks. Engineers tapped the wheels with metal rods, listening for the sound that would reveal a crack. I joined the passengers clouding toward the exit, one of thousands radiating from the station into their lives throughout the city. I looked at the faces jostling around me, listened to the unfamiliar tongue and wondered what connections might bind us, what threads might unexpectedly tie together. Somewhere amidst the gathering passengers might be a stranger whose memory would resurface at some undetermined time. Or I might pass a face already seen, long ago, and in some other place. I might recognize a limp, the tang of the sea brought in on the wind, spy a black suit and polished shoes slipping through the crowd, and at the last second see the sunlight being carried along, a dark and electric eclipse, until it vanished into the coastal air.

A Family Field Guide

OVER THE ECHOING Skype line my parents mention seeing a northern harrier on the outskirts of Ottawa. Perched on a post as they drove along, it had leaned into the air to sail off across the fields, a pearl-gray ghost slipping away. Still speaking, I pull *The Sibley Guide to the Birds of Eastern North America* from the bookcase beside me. I leaf backwards through the waders and rails, overshooting the raptors to land amidst ducks and geese before paging my way forward to find the harrier. I then press the illustration up to the webcam, trying my best to keep it steady. "That's the one," says my father, smiling back at me on the screen.

The longer I live in a different part of the world, the more thumbed this book becomes. It covers 650 species to be found in that vast and varied territory east of the Rocky Mountains, including the birds' habitat preferences, nesting behavior, and mercurial plumages, along with keys to their identification. But it's a guide to far more than birds, those unique and elegant sums of feathers and songs, flight styles and geography. It's also a book that binds, like a rope pulling the continents closer.

Back when we all lived together, none of us noticed birds, except the ones we couldn't miss. Beyond the riotous blue jays and scarlet cardinals that brought spectacle to our suburban garden, birds rarely strayed into our family's field of vision. They lived entirely on the peripheries, read about in the *National Geographic* magazines that my father shelved chronologically in the basement, or heard described by Marlin Perkins when we sat down in front of the TV to watch *Mutual of Omaha's Wild Kingdom*. But over the years we've each developed a keen interest in observing the natural world, a fascination that's grown alongside our geographical drift: my brother having ditched the suburbs for a city; my parents' retirement to rural eastern Ontario; and my own journey to Greece.

Each time we speak we talk of recent discoveries: animal tracks stippling the snow; a chrysalis seen suspended from a vine; a cloud of dragonflies about the boat. It's like being on a family excursion without leaving the line, a daytrip into the wild. But it's the birds that garner much of our attention, that lace together our worlds from afar.

The field guide lets me share in their seeing. I can know the woodpecker on my brother's walks, sense the clamor and color about the feeder, or hear the warbler in my parents' cherry tree. I can picture the ruffed grouse that sat for days on the roof of their house, its slicked-back crest and cinnamon wings. I can imagine the gaudy jaunt taken by the wood duck up the trunk of a pine, the wild turkeys plowing snow as they roam. I learn what spring brings to the river down the road, what solitary calls crack the December cold.

Just as in the field, we often fail miserably at distinguishing similar shorebirds over the phone. Juveniles rightly mystify, and when I finally give up trying to match my brother's description to any of the pictured young, we chalk the ledger of the unknown again. We experience the excitement of a sighting that the maps then pronounce impossible, or the puzzling brown bird that vanished the second it was seen. They'll remain mysteries until the end, a part of the intimacy with winged and shifting creatures. Embracing the uncertainty is a beauty we share.

Rarely do we encounter the same birds as the other, so few spanning the old world and the new. Despite the common family names of North American and European species—sandpipers, kingfishers, sparrows— we're usually observing close relatives, similar but distinct descendants. But while still on the Skype line with my parents, I look more closely at the field guide, cross-checking the Latin after reading the northern harrier description, and realize it's the same species found in Europe, though it goes by a different common name.

The northern harriers of my parents' skies are known as hen harriers over here, and a few of them winter beside the lakes, the males' pale plumage mirroring the cold gray light. I've watched them quarter stands of dry corn, wavering in wait for small birds to rise up from the feast of spilled seed. I've seen them scythe beside the reeds where they roost, and tumble from trees to disappear into dusk. And when I next glimpse one ghosting over the snows of northern Greece, I'll journey, for a moment, to the far side of the world.

On Passage

ON THE DESK where I write sits a small spice box. It is circular, and fitted with a lid that reminds me of a Chinese peasant's hat. Made from inexpensive wood, the spice box is unfinished on the inside, where a swirl of red paint makes its way around the underside of the bare lid. On the outside, the box's design is conveyed through two colors: oil-black and a worn scarlet. It is a simple, yet beautiful, motif of red sunflowers centered in black arches, surrounded by a forest of leaves. Originating in Afghanistan, the box would have held salt, pepper, or other basic spices when found in a home in that country. It is empty now, though not quite.

☼

At the end of January 2006, after a severe storm system had tapered off, Julia and I went walking. Patches of snow in the hollows lit up the land like vagrant stars. Otherwise the plain was a scattering of winter browns, arranged in the gradations of dormancy: fluffed rushes and fallen leaves, dead grass, sodden boughs. Desiccated stalks of greater mullein dotted the scrub like hundreds of standing arrows preserved from an ancient war.

The storms had originated in Siberia, bringing heavy snowfall, plunging temperatures, and fierce winds as they spread into central and southeastern Europe, over Turkey and the Caucasus. Some countries declared a state of emergency; it was the harshest weather they had experienced in a quarter of a century. Temperatures fell to minus thirty Celsius in a number of places and the bitter cold, combined with exposure, particularly amongst the elderly and the homeless, led to the loss of hundreds of lives throughout the region. The inability of rescue teams to reach isolated villages, coupled with a critical shortage of heating fuel, compounded the tragedy. In some cases it took days for people to learn their fate—they waited out the storms alone. Although parts of Greece suffered serious snowfall and power outages, Prespa had been at the very edge of the weakening gales. We'd been spared the worst.

We neared Great Prespa Lake along the winding river. The water was a pale, hazy green as it dragged and waved weeds in its undertow like hair. Otter tracks stepped out of the water and walked off into pockets of reeds unsnapped by snow. The scarlet tips of the winter-thin willows blazed in the blue sky and the downy seeds of sedges and reeds drifted on the wind, sparkling in the clear light.

The last of the river swept in a deep curve and rippled into the lake. From the slight rise of a sandbar we looked out over the shared cobalt waters. Snow was spilling down the mountain gullies of Albania, while the high, staggered peaks in FYR of Macedonia glittered white as they rose sharply from the lake. Standing on the reed-fringed southern shore, the whistling wind greeted us head-on. It was only a few precious degrees above zero, yet the fullness of the light resembled spring.

A great white egret lifted from the reeds and a handful of snipe exploded out of the marsh, rising higher and higher in their wild, zigzagging style, before parachuting with outstretched wings back to earth. We set up our telescope and began looking at the wildfowl on the lake. There were tufted ducks sporting elegantly swept-back crests, male smews wearing white robes set off by narrow ebony sashes, black-necked grebes bobbing in their dozens, and a few pochards and goosanders asleep on the water. Amongst these, and countless common coot, we noticed a group of four large brown ducks that puzzled us. They were stocky, somewhat larger than the other wildfowl, and stayed noticeably together as a group. We watched, and waited, alternating between the pages of our field guide and the telescope, studying each aspect of the birds to be sure. By the time one of the ducks reached up to shake its wings, revealing its wing panel of telltale white feathers, the temperature had slipped back beneath freezing, but we knew for certain. The birds were female velvet scoters, and strangers to this lake.

❄

In Europe the velvet scoter, *Melanitta fusca*, is predominantly a northern bird that breeds in Scandinavia, Siberia, and the coastal areas of the Baltic Sea. It tends toward the fresh waters of mountain and tundra lakes, rivers in boreal forests, and salty, brackish coasts. They make their nests on the ground, usually not far from water. This northern population, numbering about a million birds, migrates short distances south and west at the end of the breeding season to winter on the Baltic Sea and along the coasts of Norway and Denmark.

A small and isolated population of about fifteen hundred velvet scoters breeds in the Caucasus, however. This distinct group of birds nests on the mountainous plateaus of Georgia, Armenia, Azerbaijan, and southeast Turkey, often utilizing the water-filled cones of extinct volcanoes. In winter, the Caucasus's velvet scoters gather on the Black Sea off the coast of Georgia. The four birds we had seen in Prespa began their journey there, over fifteen hundred kilometers away, when the cold front of the Siberian storms sealed the rim of the Black Sea in ice.

❄

A few weeks before the storms forced the velvet scoters westwards, Julia and I set out in the opposite direction, taking the train from Thessaloníki to Istanbul. From the window of our room in the old town we could see the Bosporus Strait, and it was hard to shift our attention from the vessels that paraded endlessly along it. Colossal oil tankers, guided by toylike pilot boats, slid slowly through the waters, followed by rusting freighters of indeterminate age. There were barges piled so precariously high with steel rods, industrial cables, and pyramids of oil drums that their hulls appeared to have drowned, leaving the cargo to drift on alone. Cruise liners furrowed past, peopled with a myriad of nationalities; self-contained fish factories floated toward thinning seas; and immense container ships, laden with unguessable goods, proceeded to ports throughout the world.

Looking south from our hotel window, we could see the strait opening into the Sea of Marmara, an inland body of water that leads to the Mediterranean Sea, and then the world beyond. To the north lies the vast Black Sea and its industrial harbors, ports, fishing grounds, and oil terminals. As early as the sixteenth century, a French scholar, Petrus Gyllius, claimed that the Bosporus "surpasses all straits, because with one key it opens and closes two worlds, two seas." The vessels that passed into view of our window were following in the wake of that assertion.

The Bosporus is one of the world's busiest waterways, handling fifty thousand ships annually. This excludes the multitude of ferries, small fishing boats, and pleasure craft that constantly crisscross the strait, darting and weaving around tankers and barges, pulling up midchannel in a slow curve of foaming water to allow a larger vessel to pass. From the vantage point of a ferry the scale of a passing tanker is staggering, but for the more than thirteen million people that live in Istanbul, the sight is a way of life. Each day half a million residents of the city and its sprawling suburbs, swollen with immigrants from the Turkish interior and the neighboring Caucasus, commute between its Asian and European shores. Movement is at the heart of the city's existence.

Despite its everyday use, the Bosporus retains a sense of sovereign mystery; it is a place of strange passage. A first casual glance reveals the water rushing from north to south, as if it were being poured through the funneled mouth of the channel from the Black Sea to the Sea of Marmara, and on to the Mediterranean. This appearance, convincing though it is, is a partial illusion, as though the Bosporus were a mirror, revealing the reflected surface only. The appearance lacks both depth and dimension; it obscures intimacy. For beneath the visible current moves another.

The elevation of the Black Sea is slightly higher than that of the Sea of Marmara and, as a result, the freshwater of the first makes its way south, on the surface of the strait, through gravity. Due to differences in salinity, and therefore buoyancy, between the two bodies of water, however, there also exists a submerged salty current that runs counter to the seen, flowing northwards through the strait from the Sea of Marmara. As in all places of confluence, there is a mixing and mingling. The two currents give rise to a richly distinctive and unpredictable marine mosaic, ideally symbolized by its sheen.

In the even cast of gray light that remained constant throughout our January stay, the waters of the Bosporus seemed luminescent, as if lit from beneath by intense turquoise searchlights. The strait glowed with an otherworldly shine, like a site ordained for auguries. In classical Rome it was common for a priest, or augur, to study the flight of birds as a method of divination. Certain species were believed to be messengers of the gods, who would reveal, through the correct interpretation of their flight, the course of future events.

As I stood in the rain on the open deck of a ferry, I saw whirlpools unexpectedly appear. I watched a surging backwash, eddies riding roughly against the waves, sudden swirling turns and corkscrews in the luminous strait. It was a place of wild convergence, of rancorous nautical brawls. Shearwaters careened in tight, synchronized flocks close to the surface of the water. If ancient augurs were to have observed their flight for celestial messages, as keys to the unfolding future, they would have seen them mimic the unpredictable movements of the Bosporus itself. As if in playful imitation or strange solidarity, the birds—using the air currents that rise off the waves to aid them in their flight—would suddenly bank or pitch, gain height and then dive, swoop and weave around the boat, spiraling all the while in syncopated flight. They were made for these waters, at peace in the confusion of cardinal points.

✿

We bought the spice box as a reminder, a symbol of friendship. Drawn by its unusual design, I had picked it up moments before Rashid came out of his father's shop and introduced himself. I was still holding the spice box almost an hour later when we said good-bye to our new friend: it was meant to come home with us.

We'd been wandering through Istanbul's Grand Bazaar. Built by Sultan Mehmet in the 1500s, the Ottoman market is an enormous covered labyrinth of shops, stalls, and cafés overflowing with hawkers and traders, buyers and tourists. At some point in our meanderings, we'd unintentionally exited the bazaar and found ourselves in a cramped warren of side streets, searching for a way back in. Eventually we turned down a cobbled lane lined with antique shops. At the foot of the narrow, sloping street was an entrance leading back into the bazaar, and there, just inside the imposing stone arch, was a mound of spice boxes set out in front of a shop.

Originally from Afghanistan, Rashid was sixteen when we first met him. He is a remarkable young man, tall for his age and with the smooth facial features that speak of the Central Asian plateaus. His olive skin is set off by dark hair, and the high arches of his eyes betray his open heart, like doors kept open for strangers. Rashid was grateful for the company and conversation; he was keen to explain his presence there.

He began by going back into the shop to retrieve a book about Afghanistan. The book must have been intended for an elegant coffee table, its full-page color photographs gloriously illuminating the high passes, indigenous cultures, and rugged splendor of those elemental lands. The pages, though, were now pallid and bleached, as if the book had spent the past few years on an outdoor table at any number of wintry, secondhand stalls. The photographs still depicted the magnificent mountain ranges, the waterfalls tumbling over blue shale and scree, the herdsmen and their horses gathered at the bouldered beginnings of a river-shot gorge, but they seemed somehow distant and dislocated, as if in accord with the country's current condition. They were separated from me not by their relative exoticism, but by time. Their sepia paleness conferred on them a mantle of aging; they were slipping slowly into the past. For Rashid, however, the photographs he proudly showed us were pale rectangular echoes, both memorials and reminders, symbolic of a faded past and a clouded future.

Eventually Rashid showed us into his father's shop. Standing in sharp contrast to the muted tones of the book, it was an extravagant country of color and light. Aquamarine stone eggs nested together in wooden trays beneath serpentine coils of polished jewelry. Bracelets and necklaces of semiprecious stones were wound like glistening tendrils up silver spindles. Mother-of-pearl and lapis lazuli glinted from each and every shelf in the room. Spice boxes in varying designs were stacked in rough pyramids.

Ceremonial clothes of studded blue cloth, filigreed in silver thread, were hung neatly on a rail. I saw helmets and breastplates hammered out of polished metal, body jewelry shimmering at each end of the room, tasseled horsewhips belonging to an ancient nomadic tradition. Jade marbles and turquoise amulets depicting the evil eye gleamed from slender black boxes, watching us. In the center of the room sat a few wooden stools for customers and guests. When a circular brass tray was brought in to serve sweet steaming tea in tulip-shaped glasses, Rashid began telling us his story.

❖

Despite the quixotic attraction of augury, journeys are rarely embarked upon due to divination, or with knowledge of their eventual end. Sometimes they are undertaken out of deep curiosity, a need and desire to be part of a wider world. Often they are a practical reply to circumstance—as natural as water sloping downhill or the rhythms of the circulatory system—an obvious response to hardship and peril. Occasionally they are a leap in the dark.

We had taken the tourist ferry from the old city almost the full thirty-five kilometers of the Bosporus's length, tacking back and forth between the European and Asian shores, marveling at the ruins of empire that lined the indented coast: the opulent palaces and reaching minarets, the dilapidated wooden mansions collapsing into the strait, forts and stone towers recessed into the cypress-covered hills.

Our ferry docked in the rain at Anadolu Kavagi, the last village on the Asian shore before the Black Sea. We walked past fish restaurants hawking their trade and continued up and out of the village on a winding road, glancing over our shoulders as we gained height to look back at the sinewy strait we had just traveled. The road became steeper as it twisted beyond the last houses until eventually, high above the village, it reached the Byzantine remnants of Yoros Kalesi on the hilltop.

From the ruined ramparts we looked north for a few seconds at a time over low forested hills that fell away to the sea, before taking shelter behind clefts of rock from the piercing wind. It was a freezing howl, drawn off tundra and northern lakes, but in the brief moments that we could bear it we peered into an empty place that was the Black Sea that day. Low gray clouds hung like a layer of ash over the water. Even from the height of the ruined fort there was no perspective. Like the unseen layering of currents in the Bosporus, our vision of the Black Sea lacked depth; it was a gray abyss, wrapped in a terminal mist.

Ships were gradually appearing from out of the clouds and becoming clearer, as if I were slowly turning the focus wheel on a telescope, until they eventually emerged, ghostlike, from the fog and mist. Along the entire length of the Bosporus a long queue of tankers, barges, and container ships were slowly making their way through its windings and turns. I watched some of them reach the open sea, where they vanished into the clouds one by one. The vessels seemed to be sailing into nothingness. Even knowing that somewhere out beyond the banks of cloud the ships would fan out like a deck of cards and their foamy trails, if followed, would lead to Constanta, Odessa, and Sevastopol didn't ease my disquiet. The clouded sea suggested the nature of migration; it was a passageway to the unknown, where all journeys must begin.

When the Siberian storms arrived, the velvet scoters would have been flocked as usual off the coast of the Black Sea. The ice would have started imperceptibly at the shoreline, delicate crystals and thin glassy panes clinging to the wet sand. As the temperatures continued to fall, staying well below zero during daylight as well as night, the ice edged out, like the shadow of a slow-moving cloud passing over the water.

Unable to feed through the coastal ice, the velvet scoters were pushed toward deeper sea. Within days, the enlarging ice sheet left them in such depths that their food source was in dangerously short supply. While the snow fell heavily, driven slantwise by the piercing winds, the birds were forced to abandon their wintering grounds, pushed out of place by circumstance. They'd have had little choice but to take flight, to follow the icy crescent rim of the Black Sea, passing above the mouth of the Bosporus along the way, in search of somewhere to feed. For the few velvet scoters that appeared one morning on Great Prespa Lake in Greece, that passage took them a long way from home.

✸

Rashid and his family are Turkmens, a historically nomadic Central Asian tribe now settled, for the most part, in modern Turkmenistan. His grandparents were born in Bukhara, the ancient Silk Road capital, before fleeing in 1918 from the political violence and unrest that flared in the wake of the Russian Revolution. They traveled south, eventually crossing the Russian border to settle in northern Afghanistan, in Mazār-e Sharīf, where Rashid's parents were born. Rashid was born in the city as well, though he didn't remain there long; his parents, frustrated by the chronically poor schooling available in Afghanistan, moved the family to Pakistan.

Rashid arrived in Peshawar in 1995, when he was five, and would come to call this frontier city his home for almost a decade. It was here that he learned English, developed a deep and enduring love of cricket, and was initiated into the crossing of borders. Twice a year he and his family returned to Afghanistan to visit relatives and friends for extended periods of time. This coming and going became a theme, reminiscent of the Turkmens' nomadic ways, but torn from its traditions of free movement, interrupted by political borders.

While Rashid's family lived in Peshawar in the mid-1990s, the city began filling up with refugees fleeing the social chaos that came with the Taliban. Going back to Afghanistan became increasingly difficult. After three years of trying to earn a living in the overflowing city, Rashid's father arrived at a crossroads. He made a decision that affected them all, though to call it a decision presupposes a choice. He left his family in Pakistan and set out alone to look for work in Istanbul.

Rashid's father joined the countless other migrants from poor Turkish villages, from the fragmenting states of Central Asia and the Caucasus, who arrive daily in the metropolis; the wealthy developed world, despite its assumptions, doesn't have a monopoly on desirability. Rashid's father eventually put together enough money to rent a small shop in the old bazaar. For six years the family was separated while he worked in the city on his own, saving the shop's earnings until they could be reunited. Finally, only a year before I met Rashid while holding a spice box outside their shop, the family left Central Asia behind and moved to Istanbul.

I have traced the journey of Rashid's family across the pages of my atlas many times. It is a passage of my imagination, though for them and many others it was a voyage of necessity. For five days and nights they traveled by bus, journeying from Peshawar to their old home of Mazār-e Sharīf, and then on to Herat in the northwest of Afghanistan. From there they crossed the Iranian border and traveled to the city of Mashhad, before skirting the edge of the immense Great Salt Desert on the way to Tehran. Leaving the Iranian capital, they were soon surrounded by the deep folds of the mountains that pile up toward the Turkish border. Once over the frontier, the bus continued across the vast, parched interior of Turkey before coming to rest at the Bosporus and Istanbul. From beginning to end it is a journey of over four thousand kilometers; Rashid recalls how the bus was often full of singing and deep laughter, as well as hushed and anxious conversations as they passed through a mosaic of landscapes and cultures en route to a new life.

There isn't a moment's doubt, or the slightest hesitation in his voice, though: Rashid wants to go back. His English is good, but he speaks it in slow, trancelike tones, as if he's been numbed by his new place of living. His eyes light up, however, when he speaks of the countries and languages he has left. Rashid is unique in his family in that he speaks mostly of the past: his mother is relieved to be free of the obligation to wear a veil and at the relative ease of buying food; his father is proud of his shop and able to provide for his family again; and his younger brothers and sisters have embraced the excitement of new friends and experiences, and settled in with ease. Rashid, however, has struggled; he's found it difficult to adapt. He sees Istanbul through a lens of loss, calibrated according to missed friends and relatives, unspoken languages, lost lands.

As he works each day in the family's Grand Bazaar shop, Rashid is surrounded by a distillation of his cultural past. He proudly explains the origins of an item, its uses and function, its ceremonial purpose. His father stocks the small room by traveling each year to Afghanistan, where he buys the traditional handicrafts, like the spice box that came home with us, and has the goods shipped to Peshawar by truck, from where they are air-freighted in containers to Istanbul. Each time Rashid opens one of these boxes, his memories of home spill out.

Along with the close friendships and deep bonds that Rashid had nurtured during his years in Afghanistan and Pakistan there is something else that he greatly misses, and that is cricket. Rashid asked me a lot about the sport when we first met; I had to confess that I didn't follow it very much, and I could see the surprise in his eyes. He was incredulous and dismayed that the game wasn't a part of Turkish life, interpreting it as the final cruel blow to his resettlement. "As you know," he once told me, "I am crazy for cricket." Rashid has taught the game to some of his curious Turkish friends. Each Sunday they gather to play, along with other friends already familiar with the sport from Afghanistan, Pakistan, and India. Their playing field is an open area on the city's crowded outskirts, a series of helicopter landing pads at the edge of the Sea of Marmara. The opportunity to nurture his passion seems to have lifted Rashid's spirits, though underlying this embrace remains a deep resolve to go back the way he came.

He has elaborated his return, mapped out a journey that will take him through Afghanistan and Pakistan over the course of several months. He will do it, he says, because he is frightened of forgetting the languages he speaks, of losing the places and friends he knows. When I ask him if he is concerned about going back, he says: "I am not afraid because I feel they are my own countries." At a time when the West is consumed with the disintegration of Afghanistan and the teetering brink that is Pakistan, Rashid speaks with equanimity about his return: "Everyone misses where they're from." Rashid's longing to go back, against the grain of his family's flight, reminds me of the Bosporus: how unpredictable paths are; how solitary they can become. Even he doesn't know where the trip will ultimately take him.

❁

Ships pass by throughout the day and night on the Bosporus. It's not uncommon to be startled from sleep by the deep bellow of a foghorn or the bright beam of a lighthouse as it traces a circle through the fog-thickened night, reminding us, like the hands of a clock, that everything is passing. As Western media and politicians raise alarms about asylum seekers and economic migrants, and residents complain about the ethnic complexion of place, it is easy to forget that our world is composed of movement. Without it we would atrophy and perish.

Few journeys are either straight or foreseeable. Most more closely resemble the flight of the shearwaters, or the Bosporus itself: unpredictable, mercurial, in flux. Movement is anything but mathematic. Even the most resolute of migratory birds, returning each year along the same precise routes to ancestral nesting grounds, can easily be blown off course by storms. Our intentions are prone to deviation and distraction.

I don't know how long the velvet scoters stayed on our lake, but one day they were gone. The storms had eventually eased, and the Black Sea was unlocked from ice. The birds had heeded an inner call that would take them back the way they came, returning them to their natal places in the east. I can still recall the clear winter light on the day we found them, the cold wind that furrowed the lake as we stood watching from shore. That evening I sat and took a few notes on the birds while leafing through field guides. I stopped for a moment to pick up the spice box from the edge of the desk. I held it near the lamplight and admired its simple design. And then I lifted its wooden lid to peer inside, wondering whose hands it had known, what journeys it held.

The Wood for the Trees

IT'S STRANGELY HUMID for November, overcast and sullen with clouds. Though overcast isn't quite right—it suggests something flat and immovable, like an iron lid. In fact the gray clouds are lancing overhead, the entire sky swept up in a wild, mercurial chase. Where it briefly splinters apart I can see clear through to a higher ceiling, classic cotton balls scattershot with blue. The turquoise flakes glimmer at this distance, sparking in sequence like a string of charges, before being swiftly doused by the reassembling sky.

The beech woods rise before me, banks of tinted trees on the mountains behind our home. Having just read Richard Mabey's *Beechcombings: The Narratives of Trees*, I know that I haven't been seeing the woods as clearly as I could; I've neglected something of their essence. The book had been a gift from Julia, and the subtle wisdom of its words, along with the nature of its giving, got me thinking about how we nurture unique connections to specific people and places. So I set out for the forest with an altered sense of measure, and a renewed pair of eyes.

My own landscape inclinations lay elsewhere: in moorland, salt marsh, reed bed, and steppe. Landscapes characterized by flat expanses, by an exquisite sense of emptiness, space, and solitude. The places where I can look up or out, either at the vast ceiling of cloud and sky, or the disappearing horizon, and feel more or less the same thing: the inconsequential scale of our lives. Paradoxically, it is in those places that I feel most alive, experiencing a wild and shuddering depth to existence.

I don't get the same feeling from woodland, especially beech. If I had to choose a preferred type of forest, it would be oak. Not for the sentimental and patriotic reasons that have made it the tree of English devotion—sturdiness, durability, shipbuilding in the age of empire—but for its understory. Oak forests are extravagant with life. Stepping into an old oak wood can resemble the ornate embrace of a childhood dream, where vivid mosses vie for attention with glistening berries and scarlet hips. Lichens trail from branches like pale green curtains rustling with wind. Wildflowers spark across the seasons and honeysuckle twines high into the trees. Birds and butterflies roam densely through oak, finding a kingdom of suitable food in the varied undergrowth. It's as close as we get in Europe to the fecund mysteries of the tropical rain forests.

Beech, on the other hand, makes a silent wood. Often the only sound is of your footfalls over leaves. They are monastic realms, sheltering but a handful of creatures in comparison to oak, and far fewer flowers and plants. Beech hoards its territory, allowing little else in. Even moss often manages only a toehold on the lowest bulge of trunk, as though raising itself higher would risk upsetting the rules. It's little wonder that beech woods are often referred to as naves, or cathedrals; they lend themselves to comparison with strict, religious order, lacking the ardor of oak, the promiscuity of willow. Instead, beech occupies space with a vertical austerity. And that was the crux of the matter, the heart of what I wished to explore: the paradox of my attractions.

It occurred to me while reading *Beechcombings* that the places I'm drawn to—the moors, the steppes, the reeds—aren't so different from the beech woods. Rather than a *vertical* austerity, they are exemplars of a *horizontal* equivalent. Expansive landscapes share a kindred silence, a distinctively enigmatic emptiness. And like beech woods, they often support only a few specialized and adapted species, such as bitterns in reeds or heather on the moors. My own personal landscapes are hardly the teeming tropics—more often they are terrains of solitude and stillness. A bit like the beech woods, it would seem. Mabey's narratives of trees, and of beech in particular, highlighted for me how complex and eccentric our relationships to landscape can be. There are no clean, easy lines that connect ourselves to a place, as if we were joining up a question with its answer in a beginner's language book. The threads are often perplexing, and replete with contradictions. And like all relationships, our focus and feelings can change.

☼

The last amber leaves are being taunted by the wind. They sound riled up, rattling away like they have life in them yet. I walk a logging road that winds like a snake through the trees. A fire salamander wriggles over twigs. The hard frosts have kept it tucked into the soil, and its black and orange skin emerges smudged with earth. The first fieldfares, birds of the crystal winter cold, squabble in the high limbs, and the silence falls heavily when they flee.

With each step the forest encloses me further. Fallen leaves tumble past with the whistling wind, like they were being shuffled up by the ghosts of lost loggers. It's unnerving, though, to hear the sharp cries of a shepherd in the valley far below, the bubbling sheep bells and barking dogs, as loud and clear as if we're on a communal stroll. A raven glides by, unusually silent. I'm so used to hearing the bird's deep, trembling *gronk* that I still myself for a moment when the dark shadow passes quietly over my shoulder.

Stepping off the logging track, I climb through the dry crackle of leaves. Being within the forest is a substantially different experience to walking along the road, where I was essentially beside it, looking up or down into its depths. I'm humbled by the equal footing, the recalibration of scale and shifting perspective. Standing amidst the ranked statues of limbless trunks, beneath the arched and woven canopy, I'm suddenly aware of the forest geometry. Beech woods are more space than matter, the hollows as meaningful as the trees. Where beech maintains a monopoly, the forest is poised around a strict, monogamous code of sinuous, ghost-gray columns and elliptical leaves. Only those rare plants and tenacious trees that can tolerate the deepest shade disrupt this still, meditational tone. The canopy is so excluding of light that summer could almost pass you by.

Suspended within the forest itself are signs of the long cohabitation between our village and the woods. I imagine centuries of woodcutters floating logs over the deep sea of leaves by donkey. It's the way they still do it in these parts. One autumn when the snows arrived early, I came up here to watch them. They were a family of loggers—husband, wife, and grown children—and they worked closely with the cold, their chain saws whining across the white slopes. Snow fell glittering through the leafless woods. The donkeys stumbled down steep, slick paths, bearing hundreds of kilos of cut trees strapped to their flanks. Each time they slipped their bells rang clearly around me, but it wasn't a comforting, ceremonial sound, rather an unnerving echo of dread, a premonition of falling and snapped bones. Eventually the donkeys reached an open meadow, and one of the loggers loosened the leather straps so that the logs tumbled with a dull thud into the snow.

Every last tree has been cut at some stage in this forest, so that the regrowth has sprung back in multiple shoots from the stool. The shoots are now trees themselves—tall, slender descendants of the original beech. It's not true coppicing in the sense of cutting the trees every ten years or so for young, flexible wood, but the effect is similar. I count on average four or five new trunks supported by each base, but in places as many as a dozen cluster together. Over time they've matured into trees.

I kneel down and move my hand over a swollen beech stump that years ago budded toward the light. Touching the mottled, sapling bark suddenly reminds me of a number. When earlier in the month our winter firewood arrived from these woods, I'd rolled a few logs to one side before they'd all been split and counted up the number of rings that each had inscribed across its surface. These cross sections can be read like books, and Richard Mabey describes the annual growth rings as the "record of a tree's ecology of circumstance." I couldn't discern any wider or slimmer rings in any of the logs myself, which might have told me of an exceptionally wet season, or a long year of drought. To my untrained eyes the rings all appeared evenly spaced, perfectly proportioned circles slotted neatly inside the next. What I did arrive at, though, was a number. Each of the trees that would transform over the course of the winter into heat, smoke, and ash was about sixty years old.

For some reason I was satisfied with just the number, pleased with knowing the vintage of our warmth. On the floor of the forest, however, surrounded by the slim spires of arching trees and thickly knotted stumps, I consider the mathematics. Working backwards through the sixty years takes me to 1949. Looking again at the still and silent trees, I see the forest in an unforeseen light: the "ecology of circumstance" records more than just rain, fire, and drought.

In 1949 the Greek Civil War reached its terrible apogee, resulting in the complete depopulation of Greek Prespa. Every village was abandoned, and almost no one remained at the war's end. Along with the immense suffering, loss, and trauma caused by the conflict, a practical consequence emerged for the area's landscapes: the forests were no longer tethered to the villages.

Nestled at the foot of the beech woods, our village supported a pre–civil war population of around twenty-five hundred people instead of the hundred and fifty that it holds today. That's a lot of warmth, building materials, fodder, and cooking fuel for the forests to provide. But in 1949, when the area emptied out, the beech woods experienced a sudden, accompanying relaxation of pressure. The demand for their wealth disappeared.

I watch the tan leaves sift down and begin wondering whether these lower slopes may have been coppiced in the true sense of the word prior to the civil war, managed and harvested on a regular rhythm for slim cuttings, easy fuel, and animal feed. Although sixty years is insignificant in the life of a wood, it is long enough for young shoots to turn into towering trees. A few years after the war, the Greek government resettled the area with families from other parts of the country, and a trickle of refugees returned to their old homes, but the village never regained its earlier size. The mountain trees have had time to fill up the sky. When I slot the split beech into the wood stove and lay it on the glowing coals, I'll know something of its origins. It was born of the embers of exodus and war.

✿

Unlike isolated, lowland beeches that grow wide as well as tall, the high mountain beech aims straight for the sky with no time for middle-aged spread. To see the slender gray columns stirring with wind is to believe, however briefly, that they're being orchestrated from above. They bend and sway as one, an elegantly swooning community.

It's easy to see trees as communal, lacking individuality. We may have a favorite tree somewhere or other, but it's generally the woods that we reference. Forests have a collective pull on our imaginations, from the dark and dreamy places of fable and nursery rhyme to the iconic riches of the redwoods and the Amazon. But in *Beechcombings*, Richard Mabey also writes on behalf of a tree's personality—the characters that comprise the woodland community. He speaks of organisms, as well as organizations.

Natural pollards carry a distinctive presence in any woodland. On the lower slopes I find a few of them, beech trees cut short by elemental forces, though I can't make out whether they've been beheaded by lightning, disease, storms, or infestation. This isn't the traditional practice of pollarding, where a tree is cut regularly at the height of a few meters to provide young shoots from above and grazing beneath, without the threat of the animals consuming the valuable resource, but it produces a similar response.

Where a beech has lost its upper story, it consolidates its energies. The tree heals the splintering wound by growing a new sheath of wood, a membrane of swollen scar tissue called callus that is able to anchor the new shoots and protect the injury from insects and infection. Because of their rarity on the lower slopes, the hunchbacked deformities set the pollards apart like outcasts amongst the elegant spires. What the amputee trees reveal, however, is a remarkable resilience, instinctively resuming life in whatever unusual shape necessary.

Higher up the forest takes on an altogether different, more complex hue, and natural pollards appear with greater frequency. Nearing the 1,500-meter mark, a new tree enters the woodland equation and the beech has to settle for sharing its hoard. The silver fir is a stately conifer of stippled brown bark and needle leaves, rising straight as an arrow from its humble seed. It is the quintessence of amplitude, presiding over the forest with an unassuming force. From the vantage of the village, it appears that a dark green wedge is being driven into the heart of the beeches. Up close, this high forest drowns me in its cold mysteries.

The trees are far older across the upper reaches; they are suggestive of suspended time. Great beech spires rise to the skies, their solemn gray boles planted like ancient columns. Dying firs shed their bark, and the russet-tinged timber underneath is riddled with the work of woodpeckers. Snapped branches barricade the forest floor where young conifers have sprouted from seed, bringing a feathery emerald glow to the understory.

Where silver firs have fallen they've crashed in their entirety, their root systems heaved from the earth, exposed like a tangle of bad wiring. Beech pollards attract me like secret ruins. One has been split open like a sleeve, its hollow interior large enough to stand inside. Only a thin layer of life survives, but it is enough. The tree's living tissue, and most of the nutrient transport system, is located in the membranes nearest the protective bark, stored in the phloem, the cambium, and the sapwood. It means that a gutted beech such as this, while no longer capable of reaching the great heights of healthy trees, can carry on in the absence of its heartwood. Above the dome of twisted callus, saplings have initiated the renewal, using the place of old injury and loss as their life-sustaining base.

I reach a gap in the forest, the crisp lip of a mountain fold. The beech woods continue on the far side, but this divide is too wild for trees to thrive. A torrent courses down it, amplified to an ocean roar by the steep, auditorium-like sides of the ravine. The water drains off the alpine meadows and drops quickly through the narrow, granite chute, continuing to the village, where it will snake in front of our house in a rushing stream. I drop some beech mast into the water, and wonder if it will make it that far. The wind comes howling off the high expanses, setting the beeches swaying and whistling nearby. Their yellow leaves drift off, carried the length of the valley like flakes of gold.

I turn away from the wind, and its shrill cries gradually ease as I embrace the trees. The conifers bestow a strange quality on the woodland, a dark weight and sense of mysterious enclosure, as though I were suspended in an underwater world. The forest is "dense with time," as Richard Mabey elegantly describes it, and curiously absorbing. Ghostly, yellow-frilled fungi shelter beneath tepees of leaves. Lichens flutter like frayed ribbons from a forgotten festivity. Dead wood sinks beneath a sea of green moss, and the silence is as clear as polished ice.

Red dots begin appearing on some of the beeches, spray painted at eye-height. Even where the forest feels far wilder and secluded, the hand of man has touched its trees. I follow the red circles up a path of deep leaves, intrigued by a strange tree farther on. It's a colossal pollard beech, a monstrous deformity, and beautiful, too. The tree has been cleaved off at the three-meter mark by some natural cataclysm many decades ago. Since then it has retrenched in eccentric style. I can't even begin to link my arms around it; the whole bole is a twisted mass of ribbed and muscled wood. What's left of the tree's antiquity seems dependent on tension. Every part of it is held in careful place by a taut, inner force.

A moss-drenched buckle leans out like a gothic balcony, tilting the tree's center of gravity. Keeling over to one side, it's somehow managed to counterbalance itself with ligaments of woven wood laid off the other way and weighted with warty bulges. The beech is a gallery of inventive excrescences. The scar tissue is pleached together in complex forms, seemingly grafted into position. Among the mossy knuckles and cleft hollows are the renewing shoots, now slim trees themselves, rising confidently from a sunken crown.

Other beech trees tower around it like a protective citadel, but what's saved it from being branded with a red dot are its injuries. The pollards aren't good wood in loggers' eyes—lacking the even and dependable qualities that are the mark of fine timber. All that is ungainly, and at odds with its neighbors, commands a distinctive and preserving presence.

There is no easily discernible movement made by trees, except what the wind articulates. Even the unfurling of spring leaves is so gradual that one day, glancing through a window in passing, they are suddenly with us—pale, luminous, promising. But in the midst of the forest I am reminded that trees are constantly in motion, however slow it might be. While working my way around the massive bulk of contused scar tissue, adorned with emerald moss and an intricate fretwork of pale lichens, I sense a distinguishing spirit, endlessly flowing. The enormity of this beech's resistance, its struggle to survive, speaks clearly of that becoming. For decades it must have been producing new tissue to cover the sagging, weeping wound, almost kneeling down from the weight in order to stem the tide of insects and infection. Quietly, intently, in the looming shadows of untouched trees, it began anew.

✵

The wind picks up as I curl down the track, heading home. Beech leaves are cartwheeling past me. A few flickers of sunlight, hesitant as guesses, sparkle through the trees, and I realize that I'm smiling. I'm coming to love woods as well it seems, but slowly, more carefully, as if we were widows getting to know each other later in life. It's not the wild spell cast by moorlands and marsh, nor the enlivening rush of estuary and steppe, but a contentment, a coming to terms with the simplicities of time—the persuasive pleasures of trust, companionship, sharing. Whatever it is that compels these connections, the subjective allure of the land is a continually shifting, and enriching, inner terrain.

I descend the last bends in a dream—which isn't ideal when you're meant to be paying close attention—but sometimes the land and the seasons, the weather and the light, can do that, burrowing down toward a still, reflective point, a heartwood more essential than a tree's. Our relationships with landscapes and place are composed of such moments, whether solitary or in succession. As Ellen Meloy has written, "Perception itself is the embrace." Letting the wild world in until we're tangled up together.

Around me the forest falls. The burnished leaves and remembered snow, the shadow of the raven upon my shoulder. There's the cold water torrent and ruined spires. The autumn falling light that filters through leaves until it pools into silence. A presence at play in the trees will carry me back again, in search of other depths. I had come to the woods by way of a book, but as the path levels out beneath the vast, pursuing sky, it's the gift that I remember. I whisper my thanks through the swirl of leaves in return.

A Winter Moth

Certain things, as I am increasingly becoming aware, have a way
of returning unexpectedly, often after a lengthy absence.
    W. G. SEBALD, *The Emigrants*

A SHADOW DANCED through the room as we sat down to dinner. We traced the dark movements skittering across the pale
walls to the bulb hanging outside the window, where an unseasonable moth circled the light, projecting its silhouetted presence
deep into the room. It was December, and Julia said, "Amazing.
A winter moth."

Those three final words stayed with me. I liked the unusual-
ness of their sound, coupled with the rarity and significance of
the occasion. In recent years we'd noticed increasingly strange
animal appearances and unexpected phenomena. Our evening
visitor seemed an apt messenger for a warming and less stable climate as it twitched perilously close to the scorching bulb. Within
moments the shadow had gone, the winter moth streaking back
into the dark, enfolding night.

Shortly after Christmas, the idea of a winter moth returned to
me. I was planning a research trip to Romania, and while reading
about Bucharest I learned that the city's natural history museum
held one of the world's greatest collections of moths and butterflies. The image of the moth through the evening window circled
around me, and I decided to follow its vague trajectory by planning my journey for the end of winter.

I arrived in Bucharest expecting the city to be ground in with cold, with old gray snow slumped at the roadsides. But winter didn't materialize in the Balkan peninsula that year, nor in much of continental Europe for that matter. As I approached the Grigore Antipa Natural History Museum across the vast, sun-drenched space of the Piata Victoriei, where blackthorn and cherry trees bloomed in scented profusion, it was in every sense spring. The idea of a *winter* moth was left behind, stranded by the leapfrogging of seasons.

❉

Collections are strange creatures, beguiling hybrids: they act as both mirrors and windows. According to its contents, a collection reflects back something of the collector himself, some intangible glimpse into the quality of his fascination. But it is possible to see beyond the reflection, as well, clear through the sealed jars and viewing cases, the glass boxes and vials, into another age, the era in which they were assembled. Classical collecting was predominantly a male pursuit, and often cloaked in the associated imagery of the aristocracy, the impenetrable world of gentlemen's clubs, and casual colonialism.

Regardless of the implications of their time, collections strike many as cloying and narcissistic curiosities, empires of eccentricity. For others, though, they are repositories of a tender obsession. However they might be perceived, it is easy in the twenty-first century—an age of endless data, of millions of uploaded images and multiplying archives of video, of a vast inventory of both significant and equally trivial information available within reach of a fingertip—to see them as redolent of a bygone time, a quaint and archaic pastime that no longer sustains any purposeful meaning. But the finest collections, untainted by fetish or the power of trophies, speak of an elegant fastidiousness, a meticulous precision at odds with our contemporary, disposable culture. They restore faith in the practice of craft.

Due to lack of space and concerns for its fragility, the butterfly and moth collection of the Bucharest Natural History Museum is closed to the public, an ark stowed out of sight. Dorel Ruşti, the museum's lepidopteral curator, showed me into a small white room where I had already read that more than 120,000 specimens lay gathered beneath glass, the majority of them collected by a single man, Aristide Caradja. We could barely move within the room. Each wall, along with the floor itself, was crammed with collecting cabinets, leaving a narrow rectangular path along which to walk. The cabinets could have furnished a museum themselves. They came in a multitude of forms: trunks and sea chests; tallboys piled on top of one another; drinks cabinets and chests of drawers; great wardrobes with swinging doors. And they were made from a variety of woods, each revealing the style and shape of an individual craftsman. Their only consistency lay in their contents.

Dorel opened the doors of a random cabinet. Slotted onto wooden runners, stacked one above the other like trays in a cafeteria trolley, were a series of flat collecting cases. A strange, acrid smell that I'd been vaguely aware of since entering the room flooded out through the open doors. Dorel withdrew a case and held it close to me. It was made of cherrywood, like all the cases in the various cabinets, he said, and sealed with small brass clasps. The case was both topped and bottomed with glass so that the specimens could be studied from both sides. In the top, right-hand corner rested a white cotton pillow. It was soaked with naphthalene, Dorel told me, which explained the pervading odor—the primary ingredient in mothballs had long been used to protect the preserved insects from their living kin.

Looking through the glass, I saw dozens of colorful butterflies skewered onto pins. None of them was familiar to me. They were delicately patterned, iridescent in places. Each of the butterflies was mounted on a minute rectangular base to prevent the specimen from sliding down the pin. Today these supports would be made of foam, but each one in the collection was cut from the pliable marrow of elderberry, *Sambucus nigra*. Dorel pulled out a few more cases of small, resplendent butterflies, but I could tell his heart was leading us elsewhere.

"Just like in the wild," he said, while turning to another cabinet, "these butterflies form only a small part of the collection. Aristide Caradja's real passion was micro-moths." He led me to the largest wardrobe cabinet. We had to first open a door, then tuck ourselves into its open wing, before we had enough room to open the other. Faded photographs and newspaper clippings of eminent European naturalists graced the inside of the wood panels. I did a quick tally: the cabinet contained one hundred and fifty glass and cherrywood cases in two, neat columns.

Dorel slid out a case. Pale blue paper covered the lower glass pane this time. Above it, innumerable minute moths floated on pins. Each moth was a variation on brown: some flecked with gold, others deepening toward rust, a few bordering on beige. Some of the moths were nearly as thin as the pins that kept them aloft, and looked as delicate as filaments, ephemeral as dust.

We pulled out another case, and then another. To my untrained eyes they were replicas, but as I studied the insects more closely I became aware of a number of differences. Though the size and colors of the moths remained similar, their descriptions varied. In each case the specimens were laid out in rows and arranged according to family, genus, and species. The information had been handwritten by Aristide Caradja in black or dark blue ink on minute, tan-colored cards. The origin and date of the sample was noted— Tibet, Assam, China—and if they were types, the definitive specimen that the species was described from, or subspecies, including aberrations and variations.

One case alone contained seven hundred miniscule moths, preserved in midflight. The notation cards were the size of pencil shavings, yet I could still clearly make out the handwritten script informing me that the specimens were predominantly Asiatic in origin, that minor, nearly invisible, variations confirmed them as subspecies or localized types, and that each one of the moths suspended above the pale blue paper was almost a hundred years old.

※

At the top of the main staircase in the Bucharest Natural History Museum hang a series of oil paintings, portraits of some of the influential men who made the institution possible. The subject of one of these portraits is Aristide Caradja. The man appears solemn and serious, as he does in the few photographs I have of him—a formal response to portraiture common to the age. A thin, angular face with wide, shallow-set eyes looks back at me at all times, set off by an elegant white moustache and accompanying beard. Except for a thatch of white, professorial hair above his ears, Caradja is bald. Beyond a basic physical idea, however, the images give away little of his life.

Born in 1861 to Romanian parents in Dresden, Germany, Caradja was descended from nobility on both sides of the family. As a young man he was sent to France to study law at the university in Toulouse, his parents having firmly resisted his growing interest in studying natural history. "It was not a nice thing for a person with money, a gentleman, to do," Dorel had told me. Although Caradja eventually graduated with a doctorate in law, he secretly completed a number of natural history and biology courses after a French naturalist encouraged his emerging fascination with butter-flies and moths, so that later in life Caradja would come to describe himself as a "clandestine naturalist."

Having returned to Dresden, Caradja began the serious collecting and study of specimens that would occupy him for the rest of his life. But when his parents and brother died within a short time of one another, he decided to leave Germany to settle in his family's ancestral manor in Romania. There, in the house and parklike grounds called Grumăzești, Caradja devoted himself to his lepidopteral pursuits, using his sizable resources as a wealthy landowner to buy up entire collections and to fund research expe-ditions to remote corners of the world, the rewards of which he exhaustively studied upon their return. It was on a field trip to the Eastern Carpathians in search of specimens that he met his future wife, Matilda Greceanu, the sister of a well-known Romanian botanist. The couple married in 1889, eventually raising two boys and three girls at Grumăzești.

Biography is a difficult and uncertain exercise. Resembling a rough sketch, it can never truly reveal the interior of its subject. Vladimir Nabokov comes perhaps closest to unveiling a viable approach. Although best known as a novelist, Nabokov was also a respected lepidopterist him-self. In his luminous autobiography, *Speak, Memory*, he writes of a life richly interlaced with butterfly and moth encounters. He considered their scientific study, and the ecstatic joy he experienced when observing them in a landscape, to be his defining passion in life. Threading recollections of the insects throughout the book, he arrives finally at his definition of life writing: "The following of . . . thematic designs through one's life should be, I think, the true purpose of autobiography." Nabokov worked with repeating patterns all his life, whether in the puzzles and linguistic games of his prose, or in the netting and studying of butterfly species separated by only minor, and easily unseen, variations. He suggests that in these recurring, thematic motifs might be found the essence of a life.

By all accounts, Aristide Caradja was intensely shy. He rarely left the extensive grounds of his home, and seldom traveled. Over the course of his long and highly regarded career, credited with scientifically describing over three thousand individual species, writing the first comprehensive catalogue of Romanian moths and butterflies, and developing complex theories of evolution and migration, he never once gave a lecture or public talk. When one of the museum's directors finally convinced him to give a speech after years of pleading, Caradja phoned the night before his presentation to say that his appearance was impossible.

Along with "resting his eyes on the delicate forms and harmonious colors of butterflies," Caradja found "refuge in the world of music," according to the scientist Alexandru Marinescu. He was an extremely gifted piano player, known for his interpretations of Wagner and Beethoven. But his reclusive nature also affected his artistic talents; he could only play for himself, never for other people. Having invited a newly appointed director of the natural history museum to his rural home, Caradja prepared a program of evening music that he intended to play in honor of his guest. When dinner was completed, however, the director was politely asked to sit in an adjacent room so that Caradja could play Beethoven's sonatas unseen.

Caradja strictly ordered and mapped out in detail his days at Grumăzeşti. Despite having a devoted family surrounding him, I still imagine him as reclusive in nature. He set aside early morning for piano practice, followed by an intensive period of moth and butterfly study. After lunch, and in clement weather, Caradja spent the afternoon searching for insects in the grounds of his home, where he continually upset his gardener by insisting that the vegetation be kept long to encourage insect food and host plants. In winter, or poor weather, he substituted his outdoor meanderings with long, thoughtful strolls through the rooms and hallways of the manor.

The public halls of the Grigore Antipa Natural History Museum display over a century's worth of preserved birds and fish, insects and amphibians, reptiles and mammals. They are stuffed, pickled, dried, skinned, and pinned, covering the floors and walls, with larger mammals nudging the ceilings, and birds on the wing crowding the air. The public displays also include an extraordinary set of large butterflies and moths, their colorings and markings rivaling the most intricate of Byzantine arts. Standing before the spectacular lepidopteral cases, Dorel was sanguine. Despite the overwhelming preponderance of moths to butterflies in the wild, the public exhibit leaned heavily in favor of the latter. Dorel remarked how difficult it was to convince museum directors to occasionally showcase the ordinary over the stupendous. We quickly moved on, and I realized how little interest Dorel had for this particular display.

Later that day, I returned on my own to have a closer look at the public exhibition. The creatures enthralled me, and I peered as closely as the glass would allow. Taken individually, each butterfly or moth was a marvel of creation, a matter of belief. The striped blue crow butterfly appeared as a deep blue sky washed by stars, where the last of a burnished sunset clung to the edge of its wings. The owl butterfly—belonging to the genus *Caligo*, Latin for fog or mist—resembled a Victorian spirit photo, ghostly apparitions projected upon its screen-like wings. Its relative, the giant owl butterfly, might have been the imagined universe, its owl's eyes like vast comets rocketing through a swirl of gas and vapor toward an incandescent star. On the cream wings of the mother of pearl butterfly walked the tracks of a fox in snow. The Indian moon moth was merely a ghost, the pale skies of its wings flecked with four black crescents, aerial swifts that kept the moth's long, streamered tails floating eternal above the earth.

The glass cases were hypnotic and dreamy places, beautifully lulling worlds. I noted the names and regions of origin: Sumatra, Madagascar,

Borneo, Assam. Nothing European was displayed, certainly nothing Romanian. I could see that the collection was of significant educational value, in that the tropical showiness stood a greater chance of exciting the interest of both children and adults alike than a box of drab, brown moths, but ultimately I wearied of them. Individually they were ecstatic expressions of natural beauty, but together they seemed false and out of context, as extraordinarily mundane as much of the effortlessly retrieved riches of today's technological world. I thought of Caradja's eyes looking back at me from the oil painting in the hallway, and saw how he'd turned away from these alluring bright lights to find beauty and fulfillment in the repeated brown patterns of nearly invisible creatures.

※

While I was in the room with Caradja's moths, Dorel spoke to a member of staff who'd accompanied us. She'd nodded and then left, returning a few minutes later with two books that she set down on a wooden box in the center island. I smelled the entrancing, musty odor of antique volumes and dark libraries.

The books were bound in leather, a dark mahogany brown, etched with faded, gold-embossed letters. The collapsed bindings meant that the books sagged along their worn, tan spines. In places the leather had simply dissolved.

Obviously delicate, I wasn't sure if the books could be opened, but Dorel carefully lifted the cover of the first and turned to the title page. The black print was bold and serious: "Catalog der Lepidopteren des Palaearctischen Faunengebietes Vol. 1 and 2; Berlin 1901. By Otto Staudinger and Dr. Hans Rebel." The two volumes, it transpired, were a seminal compendium of turn-of-the-century lepidopteral study.

"These books belonged to Caradja," said Dorel. I turned to him, impressed. "Go ahead, have a look at them." It suddenly seemed odd to have traveled so far on a whim, on the deep impression left by a single phrase, chasing a winter moth. Although I had come with the expectation of viewing the collection, I had no idea I would end up looking through the collector's private books.

I leafed self-consciously through a few pages. Turning more and more of them, I began to realize that these were no ordinary reference volumes or field guides, but were in fact workbooks. The right-hand pages were printed: species names, scientific descriptions, dates and locales of specimens, geographic range. The opposing, left-hand pages, were blank, or would have been were it not for the handwritten notes that masked them. Both sides, in fact, the printed and the blank, were awash with notes, layer upon layer of observations laid down in different inks: emerald, indigo, vermillion, black.

Dorel began unraveling the books' embellishments for me, uncovering the meanings beneath. Some notes corrected inaccurate descriptions, while others were revisions. The names of new localities in which a species had been observed were recorded, as were extensions to its range. Dorel pointed out extracts from scientific papers, cross-references to other journals and corresponding page numbers; dates, landscape notes, times of pupal emergence formed a medley. While Dorel patiently talked me through this labyrinth of precise observation, I began to notice variations in the style of script.

The two volumes, Dorel explained, were never far from Caradja. He used them as continuous, daily workbooks for half a century: they recorded the process of his life. Dorel pointed out over the course of a few pages the minute, but easily legible, script that flowed in mostly green or black ink, confidently squeezed into the narrow spaces between the printed words. "Caradja began like this," said Dorel. On the same page he then drew my attention to a slightly larger handwriting, smooth but increasingly floral, and no longer wedged in the tiny printed gaps. Instead, the often red or purple cursive appeared beneath, or to the side of the print.

"And finally," said Dorel, moving his fingers toward the pale gray writing that appeared near the top of many pages, "he wrote like this." The letters were less sure, the loops large and juddery, sometimes unconnected to the previous one. "He used pencil toward the end because he was no longer sure that he wouldn't make a mistake. It's a life history here," said Dorel, carefully closing the books. Looking around me, at the miniscule, handwritten tags attached to each specimen, at the variety of cabinets depicting the evolution of an archive, purchased from different makers and markets, from different regions and trees when the previous cabinet was full, and seeing the multitude of minor moths laid out meticulously under glass, Nabokov's notion of thematic designs began to clear for me. I had the sensation that the entire room was a biography in itself.

※

By late afternoon the restaurant that Dorel and I had retired to had emptied out. The light fell behind the serried socialist blocks, submerging the room in pale shades where a few people finished a late lunch. Waiters cleared the tables, polishing them with cloths kept tucked in their pockets, or stood idly and in expectation for the evening service to begin. Quiet conversations lingered at the remaining tables.

Over lunch Dorel had explained how Caradja's collection came to be in Bucharest. Until 1944, it had been housed in its entirety in the family manor at Grumăzeşti. But in June of that year, Russian soldiers entered Romania in their push against Germany's Balkan ally. Concerned for the safety of the fragile moths and butterflies, Caradja contacted the director of the natural history museum who, through repeated pleas, convinced the Romanian minister of defense of the collection's national and scientific value. On the defense minister's direct orders, Caradja's haphazard cabinets, cherrywood cases, and lifetime of papery insects arrived in the capital after a journey of more than four hundred kilometers by poor rural road on an army gun carriage. The butterflies and moths survived subsequent direct hits on the building by Luftwaffe bombers, which destroyed many of the museum's artifacts, because someone had had the foresight to stack them in the basement.

Dorel and I continued talking long after we'd finished our meal, having quickly developed a rapport. Moving on from the purpose of my visit, we discussed Balkan history, the reign of Ceauşescu, and Dorel's longing to get back into the field. Midway through another bottle of beer, Dorel's eyes suddenly widened and he began speaking excitedly: "I've just remembered something! There's one more great Caradja story that I almost forgot to tell you. It's about a winter moth."

✺

"It was winter. We, the children, five in number, had gathered around the lamp hanging from the ceiling, casting its light over the round table in the middle of the library. We were doing our homework. My father was pacing leisurely through all the rooms, whose doors stood open for his unending walks from one end of the house to the other, his head bowed, engrossed in thought. Attracted by the light, a moth was droning around."

After Aristide Caradja's death in 1955, his daughter, Marcelle, wrote "Memories from the Life of My Father." In this short memorial she describes the difficulty of writing about someone's life when peering into the past: "life is nothing but a succession of images and impressions racing before one's mind; from these, some come out strongly, unforgettable, though they may not have been the most significant, but because they hold a crystallized moment of life encapsulated within."

Caradja's daughter evokes a remembered winter evening—the children studying beneath the lamp, her father wandering from room to room, the circling of a moth.

"Where are the figs?" Aristide Caradja suddenly asks.

One of his children tells him they haven't eaten figs for some time, but that a few might be left in the bottom of a cupboard. "Why?" one of the other children asks.

Caradja delicately lifts the moth that has fallen to the table. "Because it's from Asia Minor. This species does not live here. How would it have got here if not in a fig?"

Caradja brings the figs from the cupboard to the table. The children look on in amazement as he removes from one of the dried fruits the small papery case in which the winter moth had been stowed, and holds it shining in the lamplight.

The Circumference of a Second

for Dimitris Noulis

SOMETIMES just a few words can transport us. A friend had emailed me the first line of a seventeenth-century poem by Henry Vaughan, and I found myself reading it over and over: *I saw Eternity the other night.* I kept the words close by, like coins sewn into the cuffs of my trousers. The line contained something luminous and of great value, a mysterious depth that was difficult to articulate. It was like a lost dream remembered only by its mood. I suspected this had to do with the curious conjunction of "Eternity" with the rather commonplace "the other night"— radical in its ordinariness, as if the poet had said, "I saw Edwin the other night," or "I saw a boat the other day." Didn't a vision of such significance, of eternity itself, demand a more grandiose delivery? Clearly Henry Vaughan didn't think so.

A few days later Julia and I went looking for orchids. The lake basin is divided geologically in two. On one side, where our village nestles in the crook of an alpine valley, the land is underpinned by dark, brooding granite. The other side, however, is composed of limestone, and fits easily with the country of Greek myth—simmering, dry slopes awash with butterflies; bundles of wild thyme crushed underfoot; junipers twined like coiled lovers, rooted there for centuries. It's a place of lucid, Mediterranean light.

The parched, stony earth of the gods is home to a wild profusion of flowers. They strike out in spring for the bright, Homeric light, for a brief twirl in the splendor of the sun. Bee orchids blossomed beneath trees while electric-blue anchusa lit up the glades. We steered through a dream of colored blooms: love-in-a-mist, wild geranium, forget-me-not.

A half day later and the heat had drained us; we were tired and hungry, slipping on sand and loose stones. We had reached the ordinary lull of any walk and started back, doggedly combing the last slopes for overlooked flowers. When a nightjar rose from the earth we were only a step shy from standing on it. It lifted itself on wings the color of old leaves, hovered at knee height for a breathless second, and then arrowed off.

The nightjar spends its camouflaged days on a branch or the ground, waiting patiently for the gathering dark, when it begins hawking nocturnal insects. The bird we had startled from sleep settled on a low, leafless branch a few meters from us, blending into the wood until it was nearly invisible. It folded its scythed wings back in, which left only its dark eyes to distinguish it. Then it closed them slowly, as though having seen enough of the day, and sealed them against the light.

We left the nightjar to its dreaming and stumbled down the slope, ecstatic in the moment that had just passed—a rare glimpse, gifted to us in the midst of the everyday. The wide dirt road we came out on was hard-panned by the heat. Moving across its bare, blasted surface was a caterpillar of one of the bagworm moths. What is remarkable about these caterpillars is how they carry their homes along with them. Each tiny creature spins a silken tube around itself that it layers with fragments of debris. This one was a piece of mobile forest floor, built from bits of bark and twigs and leaves that far outsized the insect itself. The caterpillar inched across the grainy surface by extending a small length of its body, then dragging the woodland sleeve behind it in the heat. Again and again it crept forward, towing its marvelous home on miniscule legs.

I lowered myself to its height, entranced by an inconceivable life. The day suddenly stilled while I watched, held in place by the mesmeric sunlight: orchids in purple splashes across the pale slopes; the insistent insect drone; the scent of ancient junipers unfolding on the air. In that simple moment, Henry Vaughan's opening line became clear. Eternity can be anytime, any day or night, seen in the closing of a nightjar's eyes. While something as small as a bagworm's home can house the infinite.

The Small Heart of Things

THE FRAIL WARMTH of March was gone long before we reached the river. I watched the afternoon recede with the mountains, the steeply forested Carpathians shrinking in the wing mirror. Ahead of us lay villages scattered across the plain, ethnically Hungarian or Romanian, and separated by centuries of distrust. A Romanian field biologist, George Sârbu, spoke enthusiastically about his work as he drove the van. Employed by ICAS, a wildlife institute based in the Transylvanian city of Braşov, he'd agreed to show me around one of their project sites. George had chain-lit each cigarette from the last since we'd set out until smoke clouded the interior. He appreciated Marlboros for their lightness—smooth and easy chasers to the unfiltered Romanian cigarettes he smoked to mark each hour of the day.

George pointed to a village amidst fields, and we turned onto a muddy track in its direction. Timbered houses huddled around a wooden church and a maze of lanes converged at its courtyard; villagers lifted eyes from their work or suspended roadside conversations as we passed. Horses and donkeys churned the mud, and George squeezed the van past carts carrying men sporting dark fedoras and women wearing patterned head scarves.

A dog and her puppies raced from the heart of a barn when we stopped. George and his colleague, who'd sat quietly throughout the journey in the back of the van, spoke to a farmer beside a stack of straw and manure. The cold winter light slanted our way and

I held a hand over my eyes to take note of the surroundings. The fields to either side were turned for spring, the clods of dark earth veined with frost. Beyond them rose an embankment to guard against floods from the river, where the tips of alders and willows stood like masts. A plantation of poplars silvered in the mountain distance.

I had to work hard to keep up with George when he'd finished with the farmer. With a smile and a cigarette he'd bounded off as swiftly as a deer. Reaching the top of the embankment myself, I stood beside him and looked down onto a narrow and sinuous stream thickly clotted with slim trees. George turned to me with a gleam in his eyes. I suppose I'd been expecting something more, a wide and majestic river perhaps, but the scene held nothing exceptional at all. I followed George down the embankment and we plunged between trees.

☼

I was traveling to Transylvania on the premise of restitution; for the first time in nearly two hundred years beavers were navigating the rivers of Romania. The beaver has suffered a dismal history in Europe, relentlessly pursued across the centuries either to satiate the fashion for fur hats and clothing or to harvest its castoreum, an oily secretion produced by a gland beneath its tail and highly valued for its medicinal properties. Castoreum has since been shown to contain salicylic acid, the active ingredient in aspirin and a derivative of the willow bark that comprises much of the beaver's diet in some populations. But the persistence of hunters and trappers in running the animal to ground meant that supplies of fur and castoreum dwindled with the creature's numbers, until a mammal once common throughout the varied lands and waterways of Europe was essentially gone.

In recent years, the once remote possibility of again seeing the beaver across its original range has increased dramatically due to reintroduction projects carried out across the continent. Much of the effort directed toward restoring the beaver has been undertaken for the environmental benefits that accompany the animal's presence, refilling an ecological niche left empty by its extinction. By damming rivers and streams with sticks, mud, and leaves in order to raise a protective moat around its lodge, the beaver acts as an ecosystem engineer, unintentionally creating rich environments through its behavior. The watercourse is slowed by the dam, and the rising water enlarges the surface area of the river behind it into a beaver pond, a body of water ideal for an array of species.

Reintroduction projects cite increased biodiversity as one of the major benefits of beaver activity, recording improved numbers of dragonflies, aquatic plants, pond invertebrates, reptiles and amphibians, fish, waders and other birds dependent upon fish such as herons and kingfishers, along with such mammals as otters, water voles, and shrews, which profit from the beaver pond, as well. Considering that beaver dams also act as effective barriers against storm floods by releasing surge water more gradually, reduce erosion by slowing the speed of the river, and are linked to the breakdown of toxins and pesticides, which are decomposed by bacteria in the rich silt that accumulates on the bottom of a beaver pond, it's hardly surprising that, centuries after its disappearance, the beaver has come to be seen as essential to the future vitality of Europe's environmentally stressed rivers.

North American Indians have long understood the beaver's ecological importance, regarding it as a sacred center, or heart, of a landscape. Scientifically we now describe such creatures as keystone species—species that affect a great many other organisms by having a disproportionate influence on their environment in relation to their biomass. But as I traveled to Romania to see a reintroduction project being carried out on the Olt River in Transylvania, I preferred the spiritual connotations wrapped up in the idea of a sacred heart, an irrepressible force alive in the landscape.

I arrived at the ICAS offices carrying the image of a circulatory system operating in the wild, the lifeblood radiating out from a beaver's dam and pond, the ripples helping heal a land given back its heart again. Within minutes of introductions, though, I'd been shocked into dropping the carefully built image. All of my reading and preparation for the journey had coalesced into expectancy, a certainty of what I would find. But if the beaver was a sacred heart, it was in need of serious resuscitation.

Beavers construct dams in response to the sound of running water; it somehow signals to them the need to raise the water level around their homes. Unfortunately for me, and biodiversity in the river, the water of the Olt and its tributaries was too slow to send the signal. As a result, the local beavers haven't bothered building dams; creatures renowned for their industry were downsizing with the times. The biologists were honest about it when I asked: the biodiversity of the river system was poor, but the beaver wasn't about to improve it. While slow enough for the animals to neglect their talent for engineering, the water was still too fast for any kind of natural pond to form, the source of such great biodiversity where beavers are more active. After all this time the beaver was back again, but not in the manner I'd imagined.

※

I was raised on fur-trading tales. Growing up in Canada it's not unusual, beaver pelts being both the premise and original promise of the modern nation. Classes are schooled in the frontier narratives, taught tales of trappers breaking open the vast country, of trading posts bringing civilization to the wilderness, and pelts acquiring the value of currency in a land where canoes plied the rivers and lakes with a seemingly infinite supply of animal skins. At the height of a fur trade spanning three centuries, a hundred thousand beaver pelts were shipped from Canada to Europe each year. The beaver could never sustain such losses; had it not been for the rapid decline of European interest in fur hats in the mid-nineteenth century—replaced by a yearning for silk hats instead—the Canadian beaver would almost certainly have gone the way of its European relation.

Schoolroom stories of the beaver, however, had little bearing on my childhood. Since I grew up in towns and subdivisions less than an hour from Toronto, little of the country's great wilderness resonated with me. The closest I came to beavers was on the back of a nickel, or when my father conjured a home or garden project and we traveled on a Saturday to the resin-scented warehouse of Beaver Lumber Yard to load a checklist of planks and posts into the car. The natural world of the fur-trading tales was as distant as the age they evoked.

Years later, when I was living in Europe, that distance narrowed considerably when I developed a deep and abiding love of the natural world, at least as it occurred on a different continent. I found myself exploring wild places—their creatures, weathers, landscapes, and moods—a world that was entirely new to me, and increasingly essential. I can't say for certain what shifted my interest this way, but I have an inkling. In a sense I was returning to an earlier time, restoring an unsung relationship that had slipped away when I left childhood behind. Despite the quintessential and repetitive order of suburbia, I was never far from a range of fascinating places to explore. Those places, regardless of how elastic the definition, couldn't be considered truly wild, hemmed in as they were by other subdivisions and strip malls, four-lane roads with brightly lit medians, car parks, and convenience stores, but in my childhood mind they occupied whole provinces of possibility.

When my brother visited a few years ago, we sat over beers in the garden one afternoon and got talking about our childhood. Immediately noticeable was how hinged to landscapes our most vivid recollections seemed to be. We talked about the ragged edges of where we'd lived, the stream gullies and abandoned fields, the steep slope called Devil's Ditch that we perilously tobogganed in winter or skidded bikes down in summer. There were the small woods we escaped to behind the houses, the ice-ribbed creek where we sailed boats of bark. We remembered the grassy scrublands that concealed our rudimentary huts and the willow copse backdrop to spy and commando adventures, the stony ravines at the back of houses where snakes and butterflies were as common as sunshine.

Our memories revolved around place as much as people or incident; rarely the suburban ideal of neighborly lawns, in-ground swimming pools, and community ice rinks, but a mongrel land squeezed between its tidy edges. Like handed-down clothes, they were places to grow into, landscapes we owed allegiance to in the tribal ways of childhood. We learned there, away from the eyes of adults, finding our way by chance or choice, and sometimes mishap, relishing the freewheeling play of fizzing imaginations. And it was there that we encountered wonder.

Where my brother and I played wasn't perfect. Those relict lands couldn't support the diversity once present, but they offered far more than local parks: a freedom at odds with the ordered regularity of cul-de-sacs and crescents, radical in that they encouraged curiosity in our young selves. Our wild places—and we didn't know any different—were fragments, artifacts left over from development. But like a chipped arrowhead or piece of wave-sculpted driftwood, fragments can fire the imagination profoundly. I sometimes wonder who I might be today if it weren't for those unheralded places, the back lots and unkempt fields, the scraggy copses and Devil's Ditches. And I come back to this: my experience would be far less than it is.

My brother still visits our childhood towns sometimes. "You wouldn't recognize those places anymore," he said as the afternoon waned into evening. "They're all gone. Most of them are subdivisions." A quick look on Google Earth that night, tracing remembered routes that defined summer's endless days and winter's still silence, and I saw that our childhood world had vanished, was lost beneath asphalt, shops, and more houses, much as our own home must have extirpated some other wild fragment. All that remains are the names of the streets, courts, and crescents that mimic without irony what is gone. Joining the long list of the already extinct was a host of rich possibilities for engaging with the natural world.

The lands of Transylvania are as full of bears, wolves, and lynx as they are of legends. The shoehorn-shaped realm of mountains and plains is home to the densest population of large mammals west of Russia. And that is what benefited the beaver. "No one was doing anything with the smaller mammals. So we said: what about bringing the beaver back to our rivers?"

Georgeta Ionescu is responsible for the beaver reintroduction project in Transylvania, and we spoke in the ICAS office in Brașov, a beautiful and atmospheric city nestled in a bowl of beech-swept mountains. So much attention and emphasis had been placed over the years on the large mammals of Romania, along with international funding and publicity aimed at protecting their numbers and habitat, that the smaller, less exotic species went unheeded. "To feel that it was possible for the beaver to come back; that's what started it," said Georgeta. And so a handful of biologists set about amending the imbalance.

Considering the often volatile issues and competing interests surrounding the idea of animal reintroductions, the response from the residents of Transylvania was exceptionally positive. Since no one could guess that the Olt River beavers would neglect to build dams once released, people were concerned that the structures would cause flooding that could undermine railways, roads, and culverts; and that agricultural land and stands of valuable wood might be lost to submersion, or crops eaten by the beavers. Despite such worries, an overwhelming majority were in favor of seeing the beaver reintroduced when replying to questionnaires sent to residents in the region. Among farmers, thirty-four percent of whom believed the animal would cause damage, seventy percent still replied "yes" to the question of whether they would like to see the beaver returned to Transylvania. More startling was the response from foresters; although nearly sixty percent thought the beaver would inflict damage, eighty-seven percent of them agreed it should be brought back from extinction all the same.

Eight beavers were initially released on the Olt River in 1998. Coming from a population in Bavaria, Germany, they journeyed overland in crates before being quarantined for ten days. Two artificial lodges were waiting on the river, one for a pair of beavers and the other for a family, a pair transported together with its kits. The pair moved in and took an immediate liking to their new home, using it for a further year, but the family showed more discerning taste; they lasted less than twenty minutes in the human-built replica before traveling a kilometer upriver to build a lodge of their own.

Further animals were released in the following years, until the active reintroduction was halted in 2001 in the hope that the population had reached a self-sustaining level. In fact, the beavers have flourished: by 2005 53 lodges and 171 animals were present around the Olt River. More importantly, the beavers are naturally seeking new territories, colonizing other watercourses, and spreading throughout the river's tributary system, taking their place again in the interwoven web of land and water. Nearly two hundred years after its extinction in Romania, the beaver is reclaiming its historic and rightful range.

✦

The possibility of extinction can seem remote, an abstraction in human lives. Especially if the thing concerned is rarely noticed, or lacks a distinctive and attractive status. A great deal of worthwhile effort and energy goes toward protecting what's left of the vast and relatively untouched landscapes of the world, raising awareness of the wild, totemic animals that continue to dwindle across the planet, but it can mean that culturally unsung creatures and places, species lacking quantifiable benefits, or the unloved and ordinary edges of our world, are neglected as a result. In comparison to the large mammals of Transylvania, the return of the beaver might seem a minor sideshow, just like the loss of fragmented, undeveloped land could be considered of little consequence in the design of suburban space. But these smaller losses ripple great distances.

Along with the mammal's fossil data, the team at the wildlife institute studied old place-names to get a picture of the beaver's past prevalence in Romania. It revealed just how common the beaver had been, not only in numbers but in cultural connections. Tracing the word for beaver across a map of the country in the three languages that have had a historical presence there—*biber* in German, *hod* in Hungarian, and *breb* in Old Romanian—showed how the creature had crossed over into the human realm. Not only did the research uncover village names formed from the root of the word for beaver such as Hud, Brebu, and Hodos, but families who had borrowed as well, articulating their identity, place, or profession by taking the name of the animal: Brebinescu, Hodor, and Biber, among others. The names surfaced across the country in each of the languages, revealing how deeply woven the beaver was with people's lives, how common their coexistence. Lost with the beaver's demise was a way of life, a culture bound up with the natural world. It was a long relationship ultimately betrayed.

In a country where deep connections to the land and its traditions continue today, the restitution of the beaver resonates with great significance. It is not solely a species either present or absent in the landscape, but a symbol of continuity in rural life. A beaver pelt was once the traditional gift given by a Romanian husband to his wife on their wedding day, and the positive response from local people regarding the reintroduction perhaps signals a desire to restore the creature to its cultural centrality as well as to the rivers of Transylvania.

Extinction and preservation ask of us essentially the same thing: what is the meaning and measure of loss? Often it is easier to notice the first of something than it is the last. While we might articulate a deeper unease through a casual, sometimes nostalgic turn of phrase like "I haven't seen a praying mantis since I was a kid" or "I can't remember when I last saw a salamander," we inevitably get used to things not being there. Robert Michael Pyle has described a phenomenon he calls the *extinction of experience*, the "loss of common species and features in our own vicinities" that can lead to a "cycle of alienation from nature and consequent further losses." While we may adapt to the absence of things, either easily or over time, each extinction diminishes *our* lives as well; each fragment as essential as the next when attempting to understand our place on the planet. Loss lessens our shared inheritance, and the world is made inescapably smaller.

✺

Winter-red willows rode the river. Plastic bottles were corralled on the water by a fallen branch and the ground snapped with each step over brittle twigs. Within moments of arriving at the water's edge, George had knelt and splayed his fingers beside a set of tracks. I then watched his arm move slowly until it came to rest above a patch of smooth mud. A beaver had slid down the wet banks and left its characteristic tail mark like the flat of a knife drawn over icing. I knelt beside it, and saw with my own eyes the signs of restitution.

On the floor of fallen leaves a clean path had been groomed by constant use. Channels meandered through the willows, earthen grooves used by the beaver to haul branches and sticks. George spotted something farther on and he dashed ahead, skimming between trees with graceful ease. I followed and found him smiling above a chewed-off willow stump. "They're extremely clever," he said. "They practice controlled falls." The trunk had been gnawed at such an angle that the tree would have fallen directly into the river, where it is far easier for a beaver to deal with its weight. Once there it saws the tree into pieces, swimming them to shore to feed on the bark.

The lodge had none of the appearance I'd imagined. As the beavers weren't damming the stream, they'd hollowed a den out of the riverbank so that the entrance was at water level, protected by a lattice of cut saplings that covered the slope like a woven mat. Higher up the bank we found a circular divot roofed with short, bark-stripped sticks. "This is the chimney to the den," explained George. "It provides air and an emergency escape if needed, but it's too small for most predators to get through." I laid my hand on the roof and tried imagining the way down, the dark tunnel leading to the chambers where animals were holed up for the day.

While driving to another beaver site a few kilometers on, I asked George why he believed the reintroduction was important, considering that the expected benefits of the animal's activity in a wetland ecosystem were negligible in this case. He exhaled smoke from his cigarette, rough and Romanian this time, and crushed another of his sixty daily stubs into the ashtray before replying. "We have a moral duty to restore the beaver to these rivers. We destroyed it, so it's up to us to return it."

I then asked him if there had been any conflicts with landowners since the beavers had been reintroduced, whether damage had swayed public opinion against the project. I saw that gleam in his eyes again, a shine I'd already identified as leading to good news. "A few years into the project we had a call from a farmer to say that about two hundred kilos of his sugar beet crop had been eaten by beavers. I drove straight over to talk about covering his costs, but when I asked if he wanted compensation he said: 'No. If God provides for us so well, then God also provides for the beaver.'" The beaver has been well accepted in Transylvania, not as an essential component of healthy watercourses, or even for reasons of moral restitution, but simply as part of the region's rivers. Existing in a place where it belongs.

A steep-sided river carved its way through sandy soil. It meandered along the edge of a village, where an ornate wooden steeple caught the last of the light and I could hear the sound of logs being split by axe. The tower blocks of a nearby city reflected the falling sun back at us as we wandered along the top of the channel. Bramble thickets had sprung up into unruly masses, and a scraggly copse of willows rose from one bank. The landscape reminded me of my childhood places in its ragged and unremarkable essence. The beavers lived next door to busy villages; they were neighbors to farm families, working horses and dogs, roaming chickens and children at play. Smoke from a mound of smoldering rubbish drifted from the village edge, and the sound of trucks and cars carried from the road we'd just traveled. The land was plain and agricultural, though no less essential to the beaver as the lesser places I remembered were to me.

Our connections to the natural world, like the ancient ties between place-names and common organisms, don't necessarily depend on the totemically wild. They can be small and ordinary affairs, an aspect of daily lives. What is of importance is the relationship itself, the way we relate to the things of the world, be they common or rare.

When I think back to the places where I played as a child, I realize that the lack of an obvious value didn't mean one wasn't there. While unexceptional and generally dismissed by anyone other than kids, those places were like keystone species, having a disproportionate influence on my life in relation to their size in the suburban environment. And while the highly valued benefits that were expected of the reintroduced beavers haven't materialized on the Olt River, their return remains significant: for some it serves as restitution for the sins of the past; for others it restores a lost link in local traditional culture; while for the beaver itself it heralds being back where it belongs without a prerequisite of justification. The river hadn't lived up to my expectations, but in many ways it was far greater than I could have imagined.

George and I sloped down the sandy bank. Reaching the edge of the river he pointed to a spray of willow limbs leaning over the water. The lowest branch gleamed white without its bark. It straddled the river at such a height that a beaver must have hauled itself out of the water by its front paws in order to work its way along the bough, gnawing it like a cob of corn before slipping into the stream again. While the sun clipped the Carpathians, dropping us into dusk, the glimmer of the white willow above the water lasted a little longer, a steady and even pulse at the small heart of things.

Faith in a Forgotten Place

FOR SUCH A commonly used word, faith isn't easily defined. It cleaves to concepts that are shifting and difficult to pin down, stemming from as many sources as there are relationships of any kind. Our most fundamental, as well as pedestrian, connections—to people, places, and philosophies—are built upon unique articulations of the word. Faith can encompass trust, constancy, and belief, religious or otherwise. It hints at fidelity and kept promises, duty, and exactitude. At times faith might be summoned to express allegiance, honesty, and confidence, but it's mutable all the same, a word significantly narrower than its needs. But of one thing I'm sure: it can bind us to the world as easily as unfasten us with its loss.

On the far side of the lake basin is the Albanian village of Zagradec. Though I can't see the stone houses and narrow lanes themselves, tucked up on a boxwood slope behind the knuckle of a limestone hill, the view toward it never fails to stir me. It is dramatic, evocative—often drowned in a wild and compelling light. I'm not only looking at the end of a lake, but also the mysterious beginning of another country.

The Prespa wetlands, and their high, attendant mountains, are internationally renowned for the richness of their flora and fauna, their collection of Byzantine monuments. Colonies of rare water birds, including Dalmatian pelicans and pygmy cormorants, fill the sky in summer, while endemic fish species course the rivers and lakes. The white coastal cliffs are inset with obscure, Orthodox hermitages, and the island monasteries and churches are steeped in dark frescoes. An astonishing variety of wildflowers, reptiles, and butterflies also make their home in this crossroads habitat, a meeting place of alpine and Mediterranean environments.

But the Prespa region is equally well known as a crossroads of Balkan borders, shared by three countries whose territorial lines meet invisibly in the water. While most of Lesser Prespa Lake lies in Greece, the great bowl of open water throws an unexpected arm around an oak-clad mountain at its southern end. The hill slopes close in, like parallel lines running together in the distance, until only a thin finger of water touches the shore, a reed-tangled wedge belonging to Albania. That's as much as I can see from my side of the lake, a series of impressions—mountains and water continually altered by light.

But when I move closer, the image begins to clear. Anila Manelli is categorical when I ask her about living in this part of Albania. We're standing in the courtyard of a restored brick building in Zagradec, around the tip of the shore from her own village of Shuec. "It felt like the worst place on earth," she says quietly. Behind her I can see the edge of the lake, blotted with pale reeds. White egrets huddle among the stems. "There was no future for us here," she continues. "There was no work and no hope, nothing." The mountains slope darkly to the shore.

The restored building is the Zagradec Information Center, which is run by the Women's Association of Micro Prespa. Other members of the association are arriving for a meeting while we speak. Smoke curls from the chimney of the coffee shop next door, and in the muddy lane men lead donkeys laden with hay.

I notice how Anila's bright eyes keep darting away from me while she speaks. A lot is going on around the center, and her attention is divided. This is a busy time for her and the association, a mark of how far they've come.

"People have had so much faith in us. I don't know how I can ever thank them," Anila says suddenly. She smiles and hurries off, but that word, *faith*, seems to hang in the air after she's gone. People are moving about the courtyard, drinking coffee and catching up. A charm of goldfinches sparkles in a walnut tree. Putting away my notebook, I ask the translator if she thought Anila had overstated her bleak description of the area. "Not at all," she replies simply. "This was a place forgotten even by God."

☼

The mountains are imposing, a limestone ring around the finger of the lake, studded with boxwood and juniper scrub. Zagradec stands in the shadow of the scree. It's a compact village, radiating out from a single main track, the stone and cement houses molded to the curve of the hill. Water runs at the sides of the rocky lanes throughout the year, streaming from mountain springs. Chickens scrat about and scatter quickly, scrambling over mounds of manure or slipping through the willow fences that mark out the vegetable gardens. A series of brick stables huddle at the edge of the village. Throughout winter I watch them being emptied of hay, which is loaded onto donkeys or slung over shoulders in great woven baskets.

About a hundred and fifty people call Zagradec home, though from spring to late autumn that figure is significantly lower as the men journey to Greece in search of agricultural labor. The women and elderly men work the village fields instead, leaning into the donkey-drawn plow to keep the blade running deep, weeding the summer soil by hand. A few younger men stay behind to fish among the reeds, skiffing the narrow wooden boats called *stanka* over the shallow waters. This is strictly subsistence labor, however; it's the wages from Greece that keep the village afloat.

As recently as twenty years ago the thin strips of cultivated land sloping from the village to the lake were owned by the communist state. The villagers rotated between working these local fields and making a five-hour round-trip by foot to labor on a collective farm. Attendance was mandatory, and the meager payment carefully calculated for a single person to survive. With the end of Communism, the fields were divided equally among the inhabitants, but they're too small and poorly irrigated to turn a profit, and many are worked only for fodder to keep the community's indispensable donkeys alive.

On a visit to Zagradec some years ago, a group of children half followed and half showed my family around the village. Their bright-eyed curiosity mingled with bouts of giggling and high spirits. Having led us around the lanes, the children showed us their schoolroom. What was left of the windows hung like jagged glass knives in the frames. Only a handful of desks filled the musty room, so the children scrunched up to show us how they worked two or three to a table. Between them and the teacher spread a rotten hole in the floor, a four-foot-wide drop to the cellar.

It was a similar experience, Myrsini Malakou tells me, that resulted in the Society for the Protection of Prespa getting involved on the Albanian side of the lake. The SPP is a Greek nonprofit organization that has been instrumental in safeguarding the natural and cultural values of the Prespa Lakes since its founding in 1991. As the organization's director, Myrsini was the joint recipient in 2001 of the Goldman Environmental Prize for her work in the region. While on a tour of Lesser Prespa in Albania in 2004, members of the SPP's international board were extremely taken with the area, but also dismayed by its quality of life. And so the idea arose, she explains, of the organization finding a way of working with its neighbors to address the imbalance between them.

The difference a line on a map can make. According to figures published by the World Bank, the GNP of the country on one side of the lake, a member of the European Union since 1981, totaled $357 billion in 2008, though recent economic events are affecting it badly. On the other side, where membership remains a distant dream, it amounted to barely $11 billion. The statistic is stark, but the reality is worse. Leaving the country remains the most common way of trying to escape its poverty. Despite providing employment and hard currency, the persistent emigration of Albania's men and women, whether short term or permanently, deprives it of a dynamic future. Life is ebbing steadily away.

According to Myrsini, the gravest problem facing the Lesser Prespa area of Albania is its perceived lack of value. It's a place that's been forgotten right across the board, not only by God. While its inhabitants are regularly forced to leave to look elsewhere for work, regional and national politicians ignore the area in favor of places more important to the electoral rolls. Development NGOs that had been quick in the postcommunist years to bring investment and ideas to many parts of Albania, including the communities of Great Prespa Lake, haven't touched the villages of Lesser Prespa. Even environmentalists, who consider the lake basin one of Europe's most significant and varied ecosystems, are rarely found working in this part of the country. The SPP's original intention was simply to restore the crumbling schoolroom; in hindsight, the intractable bureaucratic complications that led to the idea's demise were a blessing. A single issue, whether economic, environmental, or educational, only brushes the surface of value and viability. Instead, the SPP embarked on a much deeper and more inclusive project; they bought an old building in the village and restored it using local skills as a center for ecotourism in the area. Ecotourism was seen as the most effective and pragmatic way of attaching value, through economic activity in a remote and thinly populated region, to the ecological wealth of the wetland basin. It was a way of entwining the strands of a community.

Through a series of local meetings, it was agreed that a women's association would be formed to partner the SPP and implement the various ecotourism related initiatives. Twenty-three women make up the association, which includes a president, treasurer, and secretary elected by the larger assembly. Coming from the three villages of Albanian Lesser Prespa—Zagradec, Shuec, and Rakickë—the women are knowledgeable about the area and one of the association's primary responsibilities is operating the information center.

If the guiding principle of the project is to restore value to the Lesser Prespa area, drawing together the skills, experience, and energy of both local and nonlocal people, then the brick building on the edge of Zagradec is its focus. Everything radiates from its wood-beamed interior. The Zagradec Information Center, set in a courtyard garden shaded by a canopy of grapevines, is far more than its name suggests. It contains a new schoolroom, as well as a permanent exhibition about the region. A restaurant and coffee shop anchor one end, providing meals and drinks for visitors as well as a valuable social space for the village community itself. The main office doubles up for meetings and workshops, and locally made products are displayed within. The information center is the heart of the project, a very real demonstration of long-term commitment.

Once the center was operational, the members of the association were offered computer lessons, training in financial management, and classes on the natural and cultural history of the region, spanning the three countries. They were hosted on the Greek side of the lake—meeting with producers of homemade products, restaurant owners, and local eco-guides to gain firsthand experience of the socioeconomic possibilities already in play. Dedicated to environmental education, the SPP were also looking for young, dynamic people who could be trained in the skills of guiding and would hopefully take a long-term interest in the lakes. Along with the aim of developing a viable future for the communities themselves, they have a concurrent goal of building relationships with people and organizations that will have a stake in future wetland issues. As an environmental group, the SPP has the protection of the entire lake system in mind, and their philosophy is clear: humans and nature are inseparable.

In the car with me is François Doleson, and we're waiting in a queue at the border. A French environmental educationalist, François runs the cross-border project in Zagradec on behalf of the SPP. When I ask him how many times he's made this trip since he began in 2006, he just laughs. After a short wait, we are waved through the checkpoint. Entering Albania, I am reminded of the ideological absolutes of border zones. Concrete bunkers loom from the mountain scree, rough-edged domes with empty eyes. They are a prevailing fact of the Albanian landscape, turning up in towns and fields, along rivers and beside trees. Before his death in 1985, Albania's paranoid dictator, Enver Hoxha, speckled the countryside with three-quarters of a million of these bunkers to protect against what he imagined were territorial threats. Driving along, we pass the empty husks continuously. They lend a surreal edge to the journey, relics of a misguided mind.

François isn't well. He has a hacking cough and red-rimmed eyes, but this is just the beginning of his problems for the day. We stop in a small town to pick up the project translator, who calmly hands him her notice as we pull away from the curb. In recent weeks the three original translators, who worked part-time and doubled up as eco-guides, have each left the project as well, having found full-time employment elsewhere. François has always been aware of this possibility, but for all of them to go in the same month is a significant setback, after the long hours and days of training, preparation, and building trust. François drives on through the tense silence, coughing alarmingly. I decide to keep quiet and look out the window.

It's good to see fruit trees growing on the plain, long stands of young apples and pears, knee-high grapevines. In the summer of 2000, when Julia and I first visited Albania after moving to Greece, the plain appeared desolately empty. From the end of Communism in 1992, the orchards and hillside forests were clear-cut for firewood when the state industries responsible for heating supplies shut down.

Despite the budding orchards, wood is still a major concern. Turning off the main road, we follow the long, abysmally pitted track that leads to Zagradec. Descending narrow mountain paths or riding along the edge of the track, men, women, and children lead donkeys loaded with thin trees. The paucity of the forests means that villagers resort to illegally felling smaller and smaller saplings to warm their homes in the hard winters.

We rattle over the deep, rocky wells. Abandoned agricultural terraces rise in rippled waves over the mountains. Autumn poplar leaves sparkle yellow with the wind. Riding sidesaddle on their donkeys, children haul cartloads of wild grasses and cut reeds for winter fodder. They keep to the edge of the ruined road, waving and smiling as we pass them by.

François is even less happy when we arrive in Zagradec. With the loss of the previous eco-guides, three local women are being trained to take their places. Gerta, Anita, and Leda are in their early twenties and not entirely keen about their new roles, but as members of the women's association they agreed that recruiting guides from within the community was a more dependable, long-term solution than hiring people from the cities.

François is going through the training process a second time, but this doesn't trouble him; what concerns him this morning is that the guides haven't prepared the work that I'm meant to be observing. A week earlier they were each asked to choose a series of three panels from the display in the information center and to present them to me, keeping in mind the training they'd received. Each of the panels describes some aspect of Prespa's wealth, illustrated with a series of beautifully produced photographs and drawings. Some detail the traditional, and often elaborate, fishing methods of the region, others the variety and global importance of the lakes' breeding birds, or the rich archaeological record of cave paintings and prehistoric settlements. The information boards are a vital tool for communicating the various values of the wetland basin, and François is noticeably frustrated by the morning's malaise. The young women shrug off his questions, and I can see the deep disappointment in his eyes.

A great deal changed when we crossed over from Greece. Borders not only delineate different political, religious, and territorial realities, they can determine different mindsets, cultural adaptations to historical specificity. For nearly half a century, Enver Hoxha had Albania sealed from the outside world like a time capsule. Few people came in, and to leave was an act punishable by death. When the country was finally unsealed after the fall of Communism, the effects of its ideology remained intact. The bunkers haunt the land and minds of its people still, surfacing in often-suspicious and withdrawn communities.

Unlike Greece, with its long tradition of being a visitor destination— from ancient pilgrims and nineteenth-century Romantic artists to the island hoppers of the 1970s and package tourists of today—the *idea* of a guided tour is almost impossible to fathom in much of Albania. There is no cultural precedent, no history of tourism. The residents are disbelieving at first, then quietly bemused that anyone would actually wish to visit the village, let alone listen to what they have to say about it. Since crossing the border no longer carries the penalty of death, most Albanians feel their country is little more than a departure point.

The project hopes to challenge this deep-rooted belief by highlighting the cultural and natural riches of a forgotten community, the worth of its traditional ways—to alter the perception of a place. The information center is only one method of illuminating these values; another is to get visitors into the landscape itself. Once we leave the building, the response from the guides is immediately more positive. The planned route takes us past the old brick stables heaped with hay, along a winding path through boxwood and juniper, and across an open escarpment until we reach a bird-watching platform above the lake.

Unlike in the information center, where they were faced with a series of formal panels that meant little to them, the guides become volubly enthused when outdoors; they are in their element, their place of growing up, and François stresses the importance of the guides' knowledge of home. Despite their nagging disbelief that this knowledge might be of interest to others, they eventually respond to his coaxing.

Leda finds edible plants—sorrel and wild chicory—tucked between the shrubs, and talks about the use of medicinal plants by the villagers. Gerta points to a shallow bay overgrown with reeds. It was once a place of deep water, she tells us, where they swam as children and men harbored their boats in wooden sheds after rigging nets on the lake. Anita looks to a stretch of shore. Her great-grandfather used to journey along a road that hugged the coast in Ottoman times. Travelers tethered their horses and stayed the night at a Turkish *han* that once stood beside the water. The land and the lake come alive in their voices, stories less forgotten through their telling. As much as the disappearance of bird species around the lakes would lessen biodiversity, the drift from traditional knowledge is a knock against a cultural diversity that is intimately connected to place, a measure of complex relationships.

I ask questions of the eco-guides, as I had in the information center. But here, standing on a slope between the sky and the waters, the guides are more comfortable and relaxed, forthcoming in their replies. They're at ease with the place, and their unexpected willingness to share some of its more personal aspects signals, perhaps, a growing faith in themselves. At the very least, they may recognize that their knowledge is of interest. There is strength to be found in stories, I'm reminded. As we turn back for the village a flock of pelicans rises through the falling light.

☼

A graveyard sits on the lakeside plain beneath the village, an island thicket in a sea of fields. Nearby is a small cement building, an unprepossessing, white-washed box nestled in a hedge-lined lane. I pressed close to the cob-webbed window when I first discovered it. In the gloom I made out a spill of candle wax on the inside of the sill and a quilted mural on the far wall that seemed to depict, as my eyes adjusted to the darkness, the four corners of Mecca. I removed my shoes and opened the sheet-metal door of the simple mosque, stepping inside to the squeal of a rusted hinge.

In the light of the open door the interior unfolded. One wall held the mural of Mecca, its great courtyard swelling with the faithful. A patch-work of colored rugs warmed the floor. Plastic vines coiled up the cor-ners, topped with a spray of false blooms—pink and purple in perpetuity. Something was wedged by the fake candle stand; I knelt down to find a prayer card of the Virgin Mary.

When I asked the women about the building, they told me it wasn't a mosque, although the village is nominally Muslim. "It's the *holy place*," they insisted. "Neither Muslim, Catholic, nor Orthodox—just holy." After the fall of Communism, the shrine was raised on the site of an earlier place of worship and is open for anyone to use, regardless of denomination.

Albania has a long history of religious pragmatism. Conversion to Islam was common during the Ottoman Empire, carrying additional privileges along with its adoption. Rulers throughout the ages have tended to avoid religious appeals, stressing instead the concept of Albanianism as the root of the nation's identity. In 1967, Enver Hoxha explored the idea's extremes by banning all religious observance, proclaiming Albania the world's first officially atheist state. He even went as far as banning beards throughout the land, as they were worn by imams and priests. But faith has a way of resurfacing.

I've gone back to the holy place many times. Never have I met anyone on the way, nor disturbed prayers inside. But it's always immaculately swept out, the reed broom left in a different place each time. And the plastic flow-ers keep growing. They climb and trail in shades of peach, yellow, and blue, unfurl in crimson and purple blooms, slowly engulfing the tiny room.

Faith can flourish in many forms. In the absence of traditional religious practice, many Albanians have borrowed older, more pagan rites and fur-nished them with populist touches. When I look more closely at the large window ledge, I see that it's a place of votive offerings. The sill is pooled with candle wax, the last shreds of burned wicks sealed inside. Missing a single drag, a cigarette lies on the sill as though its owner will return in a moment. A few sunflower seeds are scattered across the sill, and a solitary biscuit leans against the smoke-blackened window. Coins are sprinkled amongst the offerings, but none of them is Albanian. Instead, to honor the border gods, Greek euros are piled like stone cairns beside a trail of coffee grounds.

Borders are ubiquitous. They surround us everyday, sometimes subtly and without notice. In the car one morning with François, we discussed how the wildlife of Prespa crisscrossed the political lines all the time. "Except the bear," François pointed out. Ever since the forests were cut down in the aftermath of the Albanian state's collapse, the bear faces a territorial border that is more or less same as the political, one that reflects the lack of woodland for denning and foraging. The loss of the forests affects other species as well—woodpeckers, cyclamen, wolves—along with the humans that live without them. These borders are constantly being rewrit-ten through need or use; it's not unknown for Albanians to slip over the national boundary with a donkey to fell trees in Greece, taking enormous personal risks in order to heat their homes.

François himself is a good example of the complexity of territories. He is a French man living in Greece, while working in the English language with Albanian women. Every day he must move beyond his own personal, cultural, and linguistic borders, step out of his certainties. He admits to failure and frustration when he doesn't. While talking about the divisions in the region, Myrsini of the SPP emphasized the plurality of borders: "You can't say that the national border is more important than any other. There is a geological border here, between limestone and granite, an ecosystem border between wetland and upland. There are borders of interest and activity—the fisherman, the farmer, the environmentalist. Borders are a limit or a challenge, a restriction or an opportunity. I prefer to see them as a challenge, where differences can enrich."

With an endeavor of this scale and cultural complexity, challenges and differences are inevitable. In 2007, the SPP nearly stopped the entire project because of serious mismanagement and conflict within the women's association. I've seen the association members struggle to understand alien ways of doing things, frustrated by a reasoning that isn't their own. In private, I've seen the heavy price that François pays for his involvement. He has a wearying schedule, and gets run down by the petty grievances, worn out by the politics. But when the women's association nearly folded in 2007, the various parties involved went back to the basics, asking themselves if continuing the project was worthwhile. Despite concerns, they reaffirmed their desire to work together, feeling the project deserved more than dissolution, and eventually found a way forward. They hold a common belief, a quietly shared conviction, that the struggles are ultimately worth it. "Where there are borders," Myrsini tells me over coffee, "there are bridges."

While speaking to the Albanian women, I am aware of a few words and phrases returning again and again: self-esteem, opportunities to communicate with others, a growing confidence. Over the course of a year I've witnessed a strengthening spirit, a resilience and fortitude being channeled into practicalities that are slowly paying dividends, all without assistance from the state. Zagradec now hosts children on school visits where they learn about the villages and their traditional techniques, and play games aimed at raising environmental awareness. The members of the women's association sell teas they've gathered in the wild to visitors and shops in the area, and are being invited to speak about their work and experiences throughout the region. What is so startling about the Lesser Prespa project is how small but significant and wide-reaching changes can be affected through the dedication of a handful of individuals and organizations. The

SPP may have placed their faith in the people of Lesser Prespa, but the women of the villages have made an equally large leap; in the wake of a long history of suspicion they've embraced the idea of trust itself.

"There will come a time," Panjola Barmashi says, "when the villages will look after themselves." Panjola is the current project translator, having taken over from the translator who resigned in the car. I asked the young, committed teacher of English at a city school why she took on this job, as well. "It's more pleasure than work," she replied, being involved with people dedicated to finding a balance between livelihood and ecosystem. Panjola sees the women's association as becoming gradually more attuned to the connections between the two. "The environment is where we breathe," she says, "and people are realizing the benefits of looking after the places where they live."

One practical project under consideration by the various partners would have significant impacts on the independence, economy, and ecology of the area. It also encapsulates the aims and promise of the project itself. In the 1970s, the Albanian government diverted the Devoll River into the lake. The river, which had never been naturally connected to the lake system, suddenly flowed into Lesser Prespa in the winter and was reversed via a pumping station in summer for crop irrigation. The diversion flushed soil and sediment from the river-cutting into the Albanian corner of the lake, creating the ideal conditions for the proliferation of reeds. The density of the subsequent reed beds reduced the fish catch by hindering the spring spawning, hurting the very community that didn't reap any benefits from the distant irrigation.

Currently being studied, however, is the possibility of using reed briquettes as a fuel source. It's a known technique in some parts of the world and, according to the positive preliminary results, it could provide a renewable resource on the doorstep of the villages. The reeds would be harvested in winter, remade into fuel through an artisanal process set up and operated by the women's association, and then distributed throughout the villages. Any remaining briquettes could be sold for profit to other communities. The quality of the spawning grounds would be improved, wet-meadow bird species might increase along with the fish stocks, a source of independent employment would be secured for the region, and the pressure on scarce firewood decreased. In the long term it might even result in the regrowth of mountain forests, and woodland species extending their territories to their original range, undeterred by a line on the map. What is difficult to conceive while I consider the idea's potential is how impossible its implementation would have been until recently. The opportunity exists because the groundwork for change has been meticulously, and often painfully, laid. The bridges have already been built.

François is under no illusion when it comes to time. "This is a long-term project. Better to build slowly and make sure it's right. I've seen places where organizations throw money at a village and nothing else. When the money is gone, there is nothing again." He hopes the project will become a model of transboundary cooperation, a sustainable way to bridge differences in a single, shared place.

December in the Balkans. Rainwater pools in the mudded lanes and a cold drizzle sweeps down off the mountains. Our breaths cloud with each conversation. But it's not enough to dampen the excitement and cautious optimism of the day—the inaugural Festival of Lesser Prespa Lake. Determined to hold a celebration before the year was out, the women's association wants to showcase the information center, the new school room, and coffee shop, and to proudly display their harvest products and homemade goods. They want to mark a new beginning. Local media film the festivities while a band sets up inside the café. The flavors of wood smoke and grilled lake carp drift over the courtyard garden.

Many of the visitors are unsure what to do; they huddle in loose groups in the rain. After a while, though, some step into the information center and begin reading the panels, pointing out maps and photographs to their family and friends. Others pick up jars of quince and plum jam, handwoven rugs, and delicate beadwork, and a few go on to buy them. Petraq and Dimitra have traveled here from the city of Korçë after seeing an ad for the festival. When I ask them why they came, they reply that "nature is life," and that anything that strengthens such awareness is of value. Mapped against Albania's massive economic, social, and political concerns, the environment is low on the government's list of priorities. Which is why a day like this, explains Petraq with a smile in his eyes, organized around the themes of people and place, is a *miracle*. "There's no other word for it," he laughs. "Nothing like this ever happens in Albania."

When the formalities wind down, we all pile into the coffee shop, where the band waits at one end and platters of food are being passed around. Squeezing onto a bench, we help ourselves to salad, grilled carp and lamb, slices of goat's cheese and home-baked pies. The men tuck into foaming beer and shots of raki in gold-rimmed glasses, pull cigarettes free from pockets. The room is hazed with blue smoke.

I can see the winter mountains through the windows, seeped in gray light. The reed beds look brittle with cold, and a solitary egret hunches in the rain. Inside is the warmth of the woodstove. The musicians have kicked in, way too loud for such a small room, but nobody minds; the young men and women are sparkled up and ready to dance. When I came a month ago, very few men were here, but the harvest season in Greece has reached its end, and they've come back home with some money in their pockets.

When the first dance begins, the young leading man tucks a white handkerchief between his teeth. His black shoes are polished, his hair slicked back with gel. With the opening notes of the clarinet, he raises the cigarette in his free hand to the air.

Some of the older men and women have come straight in from the fields and stables. Mud is gummed to their boots, slivers of hay pinned like brooches to their coats. The two men next to us lean in and raise their glasses in our direction. They tend a herd of water buffalo used to manage the wet meadows on our side of the lake, and we've met them before. Today they've returned to their own village to celebrate with their family and neighbors.

The only place left to move in the room is within the dance, where the eco-guides are dressed up and wearing glitter in their hair. The dancers turn in a circle—some joining in, others dropping out—but the dance goes on regardless. The lone clarinet soars, weaving and wavering in the highest range, crying in the far corner of the room.

The dance steps are dizzying to watch. They seem anarchic to the unini-tiated, but they display an intense internal order, wild and articulate. Although the village has little material wealth, the richness of its ways runs deep. Even the young children carry these songs, these steps, inside them. The circle of the dance is the whole.

The heady excitement is obvious. For this afternoon there is life in the village. There may even be a future. The women in the association are fully aware that these are only the first steps on a difficult and unproven road. They know the men of the village are a long way from being able to give up working abroad. And for a while at least, the young guides still wish to leave the village and experience the freedoms of the city. But maybe, just maybe, they tell me, a time will come when it's possible to stay put, build-ing their lives around a shared and astonishing lake. "Our home no longer feels forgotten," Anila had said to me before the band began.

As I look around the room I catch smiles from people living on either side of the border and I realize how the image of a place can alter, how their joint persistence has resolved into change and possibility. Even if this par-ticular project were to end, a process has been set in motion so that things made different can never be quite the same again. New possibilities have been glimpsed and experienced, a world opened up.

I step out to clear my head of the cigarettes and loud music. A man walks by and smiles. He's coming up from the lake and carrying a long, double-bladed oar over his shoulder. The drizzle is like pale smoke drifting on the wind. I walk along the lane, where manure and old vegetable scraps, shreds of plastic and single shoes are rotting down in great heaps at the mud-clotted edges.

A donkey brays sharply from a field. Above the trees by the holy place twists a sinuous line of starlings, weaving as one. I watch them for a few minutes while they sweep darkly in the gray light. The clarinet needles the air behind me. As long as I watch the starlings, the flock keeps tightly together, never sheering off into solitude or confusion. Their movement defies belief, an aerial constancy that could be a trick of the light.

I turn away from the lake. I'm cold and about ready for another drink, and start back toward the music in the coffee shop. As I pass the brick stables and bare winter gardens, I wonder about the starlings above the shrine. I think of quickly turning my head to try and catch them out, see the flock breaking apart. But in the end I move on, my eyes ahead of me, one mud-slipping step at a time. I decide to keep faith in their formation.

Shifting Shadows

Cada patada tiene su sombra.
Each step has its shadow.
    Sephardic proverb

AUTUMN'S FIRST SNOW spanned the ridge, laid like a cloth over a table to hang down evenly on both sides. A thin blue sky skimmed the mountains and frost glazed the grasses on the lower slopes, worn out by summer's shimmering heat to bristle pale in the wind. The sun swung low in the sky, so that its light clipped the smooth and rounded peaks to break sharply across the meadows. The cold of the snow spilled off the ridge with the wind, wild and wintry.

While I'd lingered in the shaded valley to take a few photos and listen to the silence on my own, Julia and a friend had begun striding up a slope, edging into the sunshine and rounding an outcrop of dark granite that bulged violently from the mountainside. Already they looked small above me, pressing toward the snowline. But I'd found myself rooted to the meadow of glittering frost, where seedpods and dry stems rattled about me in the raking wind. I was thinking about the things I couldn't find.

We'd driven the high mountain road to go walking in the remote reaches of the massif, and all that time I'd looked out the window, peering closely at the passing land. The river thrummed to our right, backed by beech woods where solitary silver birches stood like candles in the dark. To our left were slopes of scattered shrubs rising sharply into the sky. I was returning to somewhere that was at the heart of my relationship to place, and keen to see what had become of it. What it might still say, in its own evocative way, about the nature of home and belonging. I was looking for a parish of reed houses in the mountains.

Over time I'd learned of the dwindling numbers of Sarakatsani shepherds moving north with their animals, and of the changing patterns of life that kept steering them toward the cities. I'd learned of a wolf attack that tore apart a flock on these same hillsides, and that the last husband and wife team living alone on the Prespa slopes had finally decamped to a house in the valley, driving the long road each day to tend to their herd so they could return to the comfort and conviviality of a village in the evenings. But what I hadn't learned from any of the circulating tales and conversations was what remained of the reed settlement itself. What traces of tenure might linger.

I hadn't seen anything resembling the hamlet as we made our way deeper into the mountain folds. In fact I could no longer recall the precise spot where I'd first glimpsed the reed huts evenly spaced in the summer sun. I kept asking if we could stop or slow down as I tried piecing together the geography of a scene dating back nearly a decade: remembering where the wooden table had stood on a flat sward of meadow; what angle I'd had on the hills as I watched Antonia bring plates heaped with food; where the sun had hung in the sky as I peered up into Giorgos's bright eyes, raising my glass to clink together with his. But nothing in the landscape suggested that anything of the Sarakatsani remained. It was as if their homes had been carted away with the last of the season's animals, journeying south together on the roads. I peered up the mountainside to see Julia and our friend climbing even farther away, and I left the valley for the slopes, shadowing their steps.

This place at the edge of three countries has sustained us for well over a decade, long enough that neither of us can say with any certainty what our precise expectations were when we arrived. The shine of innocence has been worn away by experience, so that all that was naive in us and thrillingly new has been replaced by a deeper and more shapely arrangement, in the way that hands over time fit snugly into the grooves of a favored tool. It's transformed into a sense of belonging that's instinctive; a relationship bound up with the heart and grounded from within. This place has become a part of us, and we've given something of ourselves in return—a commitment to experience it as deeply as we can.

Over the years I've come to know where tortoise tracks in spring crisscross the sandy slopes like hundreds of ancient rights of way, where cyclamen unwrap in the cool forest depths, wearing gaudy pink hats above their naked stems. I've come to know when the rogue apples along the shore ripen with a fullness of juice and when the first migrating swallows can be searched for high in the evening skies. I've come to know the shy and gentle smiles of shepherds ranging the sunlight from tree to tree, the way women weave onion stems like wreaths. But at the heart of it all, and more significant than mere knowledge, I've come to understand how so much of a home is about becoming, as, in the words of Nan Shepherd in *The Living Mountain*, "the thing to be known grows with the knowing." To be at home means finding a way of sustaining a keen and watchful engagement as both the place and I change, altering and shifting with the seasons, the light, and passing time. It sits inside me, rocking its mysteries about like a bottle at sea. But this presence is a reminder: that nothing is settled in any relationship beyond the care accorded it.

Like the glass stones of a mosaic being shaped and slotted into a meaningful design, a place can be revealed slowly, through the constant and attentive love of it. But like any love, a place can spring on you as a surprise, so that any of the countless environments we pass through can turn wondrous in a moment. Those moorlands of northern England, glimpsed through a passing window when I was a boy, have stayed with me. They call to me across the years despite the tenuousness of our initial connection, and even though I may never have another chance to live on them as I would like to, they'll remain a part of my life, as vivid as the man in a black suit on the hills above Morecambe Bay.

While our span of allotted time simply isn't enough to devote ourselves to more than a handful of specific terrains in the measured and meticulous manner made possible by long tenure, we can cultivate an openness that deepens our experience of wherever we are, for however brief a period, by fostering in each moment a constant and attentive awareness to what is there in the slanting light, within reach of our fingers, and near enough to taste. To be at home in the world is to let ourselves be drawn into its embrace.

The wind parted the long mountain grasses as I climbed to reveal slabs of dark granite flat against the slopes. I saw how lichens encrusted across their surface had labored to gain a toehold on stone that's exposed to deep snows and ice, summer's torrid sun, and the withering winds of winter. They were tiny and delicate organisms, a fragile patina of life. Some coated the stones like speckled rust, while others resembled splashes of milk or streaks of tropical greenery. Whatever their form, each had hardened and adapted into an accommodation with this stark geography, this stripped-back world of austere and desolate beauty, making a concordance with place in the process. It is the small things that make us whole, that lend substance to any place or life—the myriad minor qualities entangling into one.

The entire lake basin began to unfold the higher I climbed. The mountains took on a greater depth and perspective, so that instead of peering up the sides of steep valleys I was looking out over a sea of green ridges rippling above the shores of the lakes. The sinuous tracery of long-abandoned terraces marked the hillsides like waves. I could see the karst country in the distance, the boxwood slopes leading down to the shores of Zagradec, and the high peaks over the border where migrating butterflies had moved along their ancient routes. I could see Prespa as a whole, and I sensed amidst the rippling grasses that I wouldn't find any trace of the Sarakatsani hamlet at all. It had returned to the earth, crumbled into bits of reed chaff and dust blown easily away across the valley. But while their physical dwellings had vanished, those beautiful and transient structures were only a single measure of the Sarakatsani's connection and belonging. It was the spirit of their engagement that endured for me. The true essence of their home was the relationship they'd forged with the mountains themselves, their daily way of being there and the intimacy of their coexistence.

Clouds poured over the saddle of a hill as I neared Julia on the slope, the long white ribbon the only blemish on the sky. With my back to the sun I cast a shadow ahead of me, and I watched it shift with each step toward the snowline. It bent with my body when I turned; when I stopped it never strayed. What are shadows but the echoes of our journeys? A way of grounding us, of keeping us in touch with home wherever we go, laid across the earth like a hand on one's shoulder, steadying us in place.

For well over two and a half centuries, the Huguenot sundial on London's Brick Lane has foretold the nature of our lives. *Umbra sumus*, it says to any who lift their eyes from the street. We are shadows, cast between our beginnings and ends, ephemeral and fading, but rooted firmly while we're here in a world that unfolds with our steps. A beckoning world, graced by murmurs at every turn. Julia smiled at me from the glimmering hill and I let my shadow lead the way, knowing I was home.

ACKNOWLEDGMENTS

I am grateful to the following publications wherein parts of this book, in slightly different form, first appeared:

The Redwood Coast Review: "Shadow Grounds" (2010) and "The Distance between Us" (2010)

Three Coyotes: "Homing" (2011)

Flyway: Journal of Writing and Environment: "The Memory of Land and Water" (2010)

Southern Humanities Review: "An Accumulation of Light" (2012)

Canary: "Gifts" (2009)

The LBJ: Avian Life, Literary Arts: "Among Reeds" (2008). Reprinted by permission of *The LBJ: Avian Life, Literary Arts*, copyright © 2008 by Julian Hoffman.

Terrain.org: A Journal of the Built & Natural Environments: "Time in the Karst Country" (2011) and "Faith in a Forgotten Place" (Winner of the 2011 Terrain.org Nonfiction Prize)

The Common Online: "A Family Field Guide" (2012)

Kyoto Journal: "On Passage" (2013)

Platte Valley Review: "The Wood for the Trees" (2011)

EarthLines: "A Winter Moth" (2013) and "The Small Heart of Things" (2012)

Wild Apples: Journal of Nature, Art, and Inquiry: "The Circumference of a Second" (2010)

☼

Little did I know back when I was a boy that the to-ing and fro-ing of my parents, Ken and Pam, would play such a significant role in my life. But it has, and I'm grateful to them for opening up the world in ways I might never have imagined, for enabling me to feel at home in more than one place. My thanks and love to them both.

Over the years I've had the good fortune to have friends who've been honest as well as encouraging when reading my work, and whose conversations have lent depth and direction to this book. My deep gratitude and love to Sid Dance, Martin Stewart, Sean Flinn, and Miki Ambrózy.

I'm indebted to those whose professional experience and love of the natural world has added greatly to the stories I've told here. Without the generous gift of their time and knowledge this book would be a lesser thing: Dorel Ruşti in Bucharest; Georgeta Ionescu and George Sârbu in Transylvania; and François Doleson and Myrsini Malakou in Prespa.

A special thanks to Rashid Ahmadi for sharing his story with me, and for staying in touch about his life, his recent wedding, and his continued love of cricket. I'm extremely thankful to the staff at the Society for the Protection of Prespa, whose work in preserving the cultural and natural values of the region continues to inspire. To Panjola Barmashi, Anila Manelli, Gerta Merxhani, Anita Hyselli, and Leda Merxhani, as well as the rest of the Women's Association of Micro Prespa, my deep gratitude for giving so generously of their time over the course of a year as I learned about their world on the other side of the lake. Their hospitality was a privilege to experience.

A huge thanks to the editors of magazines and journals that have provided good homes to earlier versions of these pieces, and in particular to Brenna Dixon, Stephen Kessler, Joan Fox, and Sharon Blackie, whose vision and care brought a greater quality to the writing. And I'm tremendously honored that Elizabeth Dodd chose "Faith in a Forgotten Place" as the winner of the 2011 Terrain.org Nonfiction Prize.

Kind thanks to Barbara Rodgers for bringing the two quotations in the preface to my attention. Their words, and her consideration, have been guides throughout. And I'm grateful to Dimitris Noulis for introducing me to the work of Henry Vaughan, and for our stimulating, and sometimes beautifully anarchic, Prespa evenings.

Certain books take hold of us, and shape our lives in some way. *Prespa: A Story for Man and Nature* is such a book, inspiring us through its words and images to set off on this journey. Without it we wouldn't be here. My gratitude to Giorgos Catsadorakis for penning such a beautiful and enduring work.

Living in a small village, I have missed the conviviality of a writing community from time to time. So the discovery of a wonderfully creative group of artists, thinkers, and writers when I began writing a blog has been a great joy in recent years. I'm extremely thankful to all the readers of *Notes from Near and Far*, and for the online conversations that have deeply informed this work.

For maintaining a publishing program that is always a source of great interest and pleasure, an enormous thanks to the fine people at the University of Georgia Press. And especially to Deborah Oliver, Jon Davies, Sydney Dupre, Erin New, and Regan Huff for their meticulous work and care with this manuscript. I'm honored by the attention it has received.

Brotherly thanks to Justin for the shared reminiscences about Devil's Ditch and other childhood places, to Pete and Trudi for being such marvelous companions on Cape Kaliakra, and to B K Loren and Simmons Buntin for being so generous about this book as we've gotten to know each other by exchanging words from afar. I've had the great pleasure to share walks and conversations over the years that have each played a part in clearing a path toward home, either in Prespa or elsewhere; for their continued and essential friendship, I'd like to thank Nina and Marjan, Bruce and Judy, Glenn, Nicole, Steve and Hilary, Pixie, Ross, Marcia, Pat, Jørgen and Kirsten, Jan, Xavier and Marie-Cécile, Haris (for sharing some of the secret places of Prespa with me), Thymios, Ray, Kevin and Ruth, Germanos (though he's sadly no longer with us, the stories he told during the days and nights at his mud brick distillery as the raki trickled into a pail will long be remembered), Lisa, Sandor and Camilla, Gillie, Sjoerd and Marjolaine, Caroline, Paul and Begoña, Cindy, and Heather. And for the gracious hospitality and welcome we've been shown from the very beginning, my deepest thanks to our friends and neighbors in the villages around the lakes.

This book award came as a joyous and breathless surprise. I'm extremely thankful to the Association of Writers and Writing Programs (AWP), in partnership with the University of Georgia Press, for generously providing such an opportunity to writers at a time when it is becoming increasingly difficult to find a home for book-length works in a climate of mergers and economic struggles. Their faith in the value of writing is commendable. My thanks to Kurt Caswell for selecting this manuscript from what I'm certain was a collection of strong and compelling works. And to the final judge, Terry Tempest Williams, a writer whose wisdom and words have long been a guiding spirit and inspiration to me, my deepest gratitude.

Finally, at the heart of it all, my thanks to Julia. This book wouldn't have been possible without her. Along with being the first editor of these words, she has shared with me the wonder of discovering this remarkable part of the world. Even when I traveled alone, we journeyed together.